VIKKI KOPLICK

SACRED ANIMAL ACTIVISM

A MISSION OF LOVE FOR ANIMALS

Copyright © 2022 Vikki Koplick

ISBN: 978-1-922788-65-8 (paperback edition)
Published by Vivid Publishing
A division of Fontaine Publishing Group
P.O. Box 948, Fremantle
Western Australia 6959
www.vividpublishing.com.au

A catalogue record for this
book is available from the
National Library of Australia

This book is dedicated to my
younger self, who wanted to save the world
by helping our amazing and beautiful
animals.

CONTENTS

ACKNOWLEDGEMENTS

I would like to acknowledge and thank the following people.

My husband and children, for their constant love, support and endless patience throughout this whole creative process, for allowing me the space to grow and learn to write a book.

Shakti Durga, aka Kim S Durga, for being an inspiration to my soul in her journey. I can never thank her enough for her books, LIFT meditations and seminars, music and energy modality IYS therapy. School Shanti Mission, for all the classes and practical knowledge at the animal healing clinic, which helped me become an energy healer for animals.

I would also like to acknowledge the wonderful community of teachers, healers, classmates and friends who have been on this journey with me.

To my friend Maureen: thank you for your support, and the unity we share in our dream for energy healings to be part of mainstream pet care. The many chats we had kept me going while I was writing this book. Your never-ending gentle, loving nature towards animals inspires me every time we get together. From the moment we met we have been kindred spirits in our love of animals.

I wish to acknowledge the hard work of Veronica (Sri Yantra) in editing my manuscript, which was a huge job. Thank you for answering the endless questions and offering the wealth of your literature knowledge and experience. Thank you for holding my hand through different stages of the writing. For helping know where to put everything and what was next on the endless things to do before sending it to a publisher. Thank you for all the energy healings, where the idea of writing a book first began. Your belief in my ability to write this book was the biggest reason I felt I could take this huge step and learn-as-I-go approach to all the things involved in becoming an author and publishing. There was so much more to it than I could have imagined when I started the book; I have learned much from this whole process thanks to your patience with a beginner, when you are used to writers and poets with way more experience.

I also would like to thank Bhu Devi and Bhavani Ma for the proofreading and formatting they did for the second draft. In the process you all taught me much about the editing process, which I was able to use to prepare my individual poems for the magazines that published them.

I would like to acknowledge the other offers of

help and the constant encouragement from many of my friends and the Shanti Mission community. Being able to share the stages I was up to with the book has keep me going. But most of all, it held me accountable. I met my targets. When I was ready to let it gather dust I remembered the people who had given of their time freely to support my work. Thank you to Laxmi Maa for my first ever energy healing, and to all the other great healers over the last eight years. Thank you to Justine Lloyd for my awesome recent healings. Thank you to my buddies Kerrie and Gabriella Grace for your constant belief that I would publish and be successful.

Thank you to Sadie, aka Shakti Ma, my soul sister who has been on this journey with me for nearly 20 years. When our children were young, the endless conversations we had about all things spiritual. You were with me at the Bodhi Festival, where the journey started. You listened endlessly while I tried to speak the truth of the book, hearing it from my inner guidance. Trying to anchor it as more than a fleeting concept into something tangible I would eventually write.

This book has been a learning experience and I could not have done it without my village of supporters.

I would also like to acknowledge every horse, dog and cat I have ever loved and practised energy healing on. I would like to also thank those who allowed me to do healings on their beautiful fur babies.

I would love to acknowledge those who joined

my online community page "A Mission of Love for Animals", and groups, "A Mission of Love for Animals (Prayers, Meditation, Love)" and "Vikki Koplick Distance Energy Healer". The posts I share with these groups have been my school for writing. In fact, when I was stumped during this process, I would see what was happening in the world on social media and write a post about it, and that would move the book forward. Several posts I put up on the page were put in the book. I wanted this book to be for animal lovers and to be relevant to what is happening in the world now, with animals as a way to help heal our hearts. Hearts which feel broken from the suffering of animals. In fact, in that we are one, aren't we? When animals suffer, we suffer along with them.

I would like to thank my beta readers and supporters, Devaki Martin, Angelica Hing and Maureen, who helped me believe in my ability to write by your great feedback and kind words of encouragement in the final stages before publishing.

I would like to thank Claire Bradshaw for her wonderful editing and proofreading in preparing this book for publishing. Also thank you to Fontaine Publishing for the great job your team did in creating a great cover, an amazing-looking book, and distribution worldwide.

Last but not least, I would like to thank and acknowledge that little hero child inside myself, who wanted to save the world by helping all the animals.

CRYING OF SEPARATION

But still, I don't feel the connection I am searching for
outside of myself.
Not daring to believe I am the divine I am looking for, no
separation at all.
I still feel separate from the oneness I cannot describe or
understand.
Because I think I am a woman,
Yet deep down I feel the rising of my understanding,
As my awe of all that is unfolds around my heart.
In wonder, like a child, I search for that hidden treasure.
Whatever it is I do not know.
I hear the call deep down, lifting me higher, to envelop it all.
To remember once more that divine call of devotion.
The sweetest song of my heart.
The call to be more of myself than I could dare imagine.
I join once more to the connection within.
The divine wall is down, we are together.
We breathe as one in the unity of now.
We are forever tall together, stronger than ever before.
What a journey we live,
Once more together, in one heart expanding,
Together. separate no more.

INTRODUCTION

ONE

IN THE BEGINNING

I've always been interested in the great question: *Why am I here?*

Growing up in the 1960s and 1970s in middle-class Australia didn't really prepare me for the spiritual interest that would later become an obsession of mine. Although it did give me lots of time to have fun in nature. As a child, I made mud pies and rolled in the grass, getting sticky grass seeds all over me. I swam and explored the creeks and the bush. I wanted to ride every horse I saw, and my passion was so fierce, I was determined to find any way I could to get into the saddle.

At twelve years old, I got my first horse, and I looked after it myself. I didn't palm it off on my parents to do it for me. I researched what kind of feed to use. I worked hard and competed at pony club and jump club. The afternoons I spent in the company of nature and my horses were priceless.

I shared my passion for horses with my cousin, Kim, and we spent most of our time together talking about our mutual love for our horses, as well as any upcoming competitions. One day, we sat in nature, having a rest after riding, and my cousin asked, "What are you going to be when you grow up?" I knew she wanted to be a lawyer, and I wanted to be a veterinarian. We agreed I would save all the animals, and she would save all the people. I was as serious as any twelve-year-old could be, and I'm sure I believed I was going to grow up be a veterinarian and help save the world.

In hindsight, I can see that what actually occurred on that day, dreaming with my cousin, was that I had promised the universe I would serve the world as a light worker. At the age of twelve, I had no idea that was what my soul wanted to do. Who knew that Kim would be one of my teachers and that we would share this amazing spiritual journey in the future? There were so many signs everywhere, yet we could not understand them. For example, when the truck full of cows pooped on the front of my aunt's car when we were in it, Kim and I only laughed at the absurdity of it. It wasn't until much later that I learned this would be seen as a blessing in the Hindu tradition.

In Year Ten I didn't have the marks to go on to Year Eleven and Twelve, so I made the decision to leave school rather than go on to university to be a veterinarian. Although it was the right decision, I didn't know what I was going to do once my dream of becoming a vet was over. How would I save the animals? I considered becoming a vet assistant, but that didn't happen. Instead, I worked in my mum's sandwich shop for a few years. Then the opportunity to train as an Enrolled Nurse arose, so I chose to help people instead.

Meanwhile, my cousin did become a lawyer. Although we both became individually interested in spirituality and had a few conversations about the New Age movement in the early 1990s, we didn't see each other again until 2012.

When I began high school, I started to feel even more shy and frightened of others, and the teasing was relentless. I would arrive home with a headache from both eye strain and the stress of being teased. No one could console my pain or feelings of rejection, so I would often go to my room to cry. It was in those moments when I would hear a soft, loving voice. It seemed to be coming from deep within myself. The voice told me I was loved, and that the things the other kids said were wrong. I found this very comforting and discovered self-approval in those moments. I could dream of a future without being teased. I could read and listen to music. After a good emotional release, I could feel a presence that I can only describe as unconditional love. I didn't know what that presence was in the physical sense. It felt like it could be divine. Later, I came to realise it was my higher self, my soul speaking as a divine parent to the frightened child within my emotional body.

One ritual I had to soothe myself was to clean my golden mare-and-foal lamp. As I wiped the smooth contours of the base, I would hear the comforting words from my inner parent telling me I was loved and right and good.

Don't worry about those who tease you. They are wrong about you. This voice got me through many nights of feeling not good enough.

I knew the divine existed within me, but I did not like religion. Back in my social group in the 1970s, there was a lot of pressure to choose only one religion to follow. Even at school we could only study the religion we personally followed. They wouldn't let us into scripture class if we weren't a member of the religion they were teaching. Even then, I used to think, *how do I know what religion I am if I don't get to study them all?*

I would pray to God: *I know you are there. I love you, but not these religions, an invention of mankind.* Although my relationships with Mother Earth and God were good, I kept my faith secret because I didn't want to go to church to be browbeaten by the limited views of others. How could I explain my deep connection to the divine? I knew I had it but was unable to express it. I loved Krishna, a cardinal deity of Hinduism, even though I didn't know the first thing about him. Every time I heard the words "Hari Krishna", I would dance around, saying them over and over.

I had my own relationship with the story of

Jesus, and developed a deep sense of gratitude for his teachings and sacrifice. He was explaining what I felt and heard.

I was a very angry child and I still have anger issues. It was, and still can be, my way of coping with fear. As a child, I often felt I was the worst person in my family because I lost my temper so much. But during this time, in addition to my relationship to faith, I began to realise I had the gift of being able to read other people's energy, even when it didn't match what they were saying. I didn't know it then, but I was an empath and clairvoyant. As an empath, I can pick up anger from people and places around me.

When my soul wanted my attention and to teach me something, it was like listening to my inner voice. One thing I remember (how could I forget something so weird?) happened when I was thirteen years old. I heard the sky tell me, *"Have a good look at the colour blue I am, because this is the last time you can see this dark blue colour. My colour will be lighter, as there is now a hole in the ozone layer."* I remember thinking to myself, *what is an ozone layer?* It seemed like nature itself was speaking within my being.

I felt like a victim for most of my childhood, except for the respite my inner connection provided. This divine presence ensured I could not only be myself but intuit many changes that would happen through the decades before they happened. My intuition has always been clear. Ignoring my intuitive guidance was nearly impossible, as was trying to explain any of this to anyone at that stage in my life.

Sometimes my intuition was so correct it scared me. One day, my parents' car went past the paddock while I was riding my horse. I took one look at that car and knew they were taking my dog, Sam, away because he had been run over after getting out of the open fence. How could I have known this? When I got home, I saw my mother's red eyes and didn't need to be told he was gone. The burden of this kind of intuition was overwhelming.

I just wanted to be a normal person who didn't hear weird information when I didn't ask. People often lose this ability when they are young, but I had to actively stop it myself by blocking it out.

By the time I was a young adult in the 1990s, I was nothing like the child I had once been. I had become a bitter, nasty person, who thought other people were cruel and clueless. I was a lost soul. I didn't want to save the world anymore. I thought people were doomed to destroy themselves. Global warming was endangering the environment, and people were cruel to animals.

I was consumed with the doom and gloom of imagining what my kids' and grandkids' lives would be like – with the number of ruthless people greedily taking every mineral, crystal, precious stone and drop of water; with mining ruining waterways and rainforests being cut down, destroying all animal habitats. I was furious about the future life of our children being stolen by greed and human pollution. People were killing nature, and I was angry.

Nature was my friend, and I couldn't bear the thought of what has happening to it. I had become numb and angry about the planet and animals I loved. Furthermore, as a nurse, I saw lots of suffering – people with many physical disabilities and illnesses. Knowing about the suffering of our physical bodies left me wondering how any of us were alive.

In the late 1990s, while looking after my baby son, I started searching for answers to those questions, like many others were doing. I was regularly going to the library to seek out all the New Age books I could find. Then I started borrowing meditation CDs. I loved to mediate, and in fact I always considered horse riding a form of meditation. (This applies to any sport, really, and any way that shuts down the chatter in the mind and lets you go within to hear answers to your questions.) My quest to learn who I was and why I was here still drove my search. I read plenty of books, but it was still theory. I knew there had to be a way to connect to the universal energy to help my health and life become better.

I was so frustrated that I couldn't understand how, even though we were made of flesh and bone, that was an illusion, because quantum science had shown that we were made of mostly space and protons of energy. Then there was my guidance of soul and universal consciousness. While everyone was seeing themselves as a separate being from Earth, I was aware of no separation. When we look at Earth from a plane, do we see ourselves waving here, thinking *I am separate to Earth*? This drove my quest.

If I was part of the planet, then I was part of the whole universe. The space inside my body was not separate to the space around my body. That was an illusion. In space we are one. But I still didn't have much knowledge of the energy that flows through the protons in that space. Surely this must be the chi I felt in doing tai chi exercises. The universal consciousness. The energy that created and was the Big Bang. The whole thing was exciting, my new quest – or obsession, really. I had already done all the television science shows. I knew there was an energy field and energy flowing through it. That the only reason I could feel my body was because my finger was the same vibration as the rest of my body.

I knew the physical world had many layers to it: the solid, liquid and gas parts of Earth and our bodies. The flesh and bones and what we see at a microscopic level. So why wouldn't who I was have layers? I kept looking for a way to tie them together. How was it that sometimes I was so aware of things that were about to happen? How did I just *know* things, and hear nature *speaking*? Whose was the soothing voice I heard in my times of stress? Who was it that helped me self-soothe?

I heard about opening the third eye. I would

imagine I could open my third eye, and I would see a bluish light when I had my eyes shut. This become my new way to connect within. I also started writing; I wrote down all the things I wished I had said to those who never listened to me.

In 2012, I went to a festival that introduced me to the knowledge of the Bhakti yoga tradition. I was particularly intrigued by this tradition and other devotional practices. There were ancient traditions that talked about moving energy. I was about to discover how to read my energy body; how to grow and expand into new ways of helping animals in a real way, using my energy body. The Bodhi Festival held by Shanti Mission in Newcastle in 2012 was about to show me how to make practical sense of the spiritual concepts I was so preoccupied with.

I had already attended tai chi exercises and had felt the chi, the subtle energy. I knew when I felt good energy and bad and when a nasty being was around me. I was an empath and a clairvoyant in four of the ways: I could see, hear, smell and know things. I was an animal medium and highly intuitive. At this time, it was all just starting to make sense.

I felt I had been preparing for this all my life. It was evident to me, after attending the Bodhi Festival and finding Shanti Mission and its founder Kim (Shakti Durga), that I had been preparing for this for thousands of lifetimes. Well, at least my soul had been preparing. I knew my soul was leading me somewhere and this one step was a huge leap across the abyss. Many burning questions began to be answered in the most beautiful ways. I would have never, ever thought it possible.

Having LIFT Meditation and Ignite Your Spirit (IYS) therapy, and learning to do this form of healing on my own chakras, helped my health. The seminars helped me to understand myself better, take more responsibility for what I was doing and saying. Many things I learned helped me feel more empowered as a person in all circumstances. The rituals and blessings, chants and mantras pulled in higher vibration energy, which lifted my outlook from arrogance and *not enough* to feeling more empowered.

PART ONE

FINDING MY PATH TO HEALING

TWO

SOUL FAMILY

I was looking through *The Star*, a local newspaper, and staring back at me was my cousin, Kim Fraser. Only the advertisement said, "Join Spiritual Teacher Shakti Durga".[1] There were Peace Angels, music, stalls for books and offers of holistic treatments; talks about peace and Bhakti yoga, which was about devotion and chants and mantras, and talks about energy being Shakti.

It was a three-day festival. I bought my ticket online and thought I might go and check out what my cousin was up to, and see the Angels. But I wasn't ready for the amazing world I was about to enter, and I tried in lots of ways to resist going.

I wasn't sure what to expect, so I went up to Newcastle Beach where the Peace Angels were doing a ceremony with bells and chants. It was such a beautiful sight, seeing people dressed up as angels on a beach I had been to so many times. We then all walked in a magical parade following the Peace Angels down the mall to the venue for the festival, the old David Jones store.

After the walk, Kim and others from Shanti Mission were up on a stage, singing music I had never heard before, and I loved it. It felt amazing. I had a look around and was excited about finding out more the next day. On Saturday I went to the festival lectures and listened to more music. I learned this music was called *kirtan*.

Kirtan music is a call-and-response chanting of the names of the divine we hear in mantras and chants. This energy felt great – very expansive; it seemed to connect us through the heart. Much like when you hear someone singing with their whole heart, it brings up lots of emotions, crying from the sweetness or the sorrow it touches inside. Sometimes the joy is amazing and I feel like dancing.

I kept walking past the Peace Angels standing in the windows and inside the venue, blessing people with their eyes at the festival. I thought to myself: *Are they really people or angels?* Then I thought, *how come I know what angels look like?* I found out later that the Peace Angels connect to the angel realm in meditation and connect their hearts together before they come out as a group to embody as much of the angel energy as they can.

On Saturday evening I was very tired and a little

confused, but I was excited to come back for a satsang the next day and sample a healing offered for free. Whatever that was, it sounded good. A satsang is a meditation with music and sometimes a discourse, like a download of guidance for the gathered group. It's amazing how it seems to be just what you need to hear, how it feels like the teacher is speaking directly to you. It's amazing how the questions that have been rolling around in your consciousness start to be answered.

My first ever satsang was great. I was sitting and watching family on stage doing their thing, and it was very new and interesting to my soul. After the satsang I went to many more lectures about peace and spiritual tools. I booked in for the sample Ignite Your Spirit healing that was being offered, once again not knowing what to expect.

The healer, was lovely, and I felt comfortable somehow, even though I was sitting around heaps of people with my eyes shut. She explained that she would not be touching me, but sweeping my energy body and measuring my chakras. She said that the solar plexus chakra was the worst one and asked if she could work on that. I said, "Yes, of course – my stomach area always feels painful, or like I have butterflies or want to be sick."

Then she started sweeping. I felt light and comfortable in my stomach area, and as she added energy to my solar plexus chakra, I was floating in peace for the first time in my life in that part of my body. I asked her how long this feeling would last. I was told the healing effect would continue for approximately two weeks. I was then told about the seminars that were starting in two weeks to learn how to do this sweeping of the chakras.

I felt great! Finally, I had found something spiritual that I could feel physically healing my body and emotional pain. This was practical spiritual wisdom and knowledge.

THREE

PATH OF DEVOTION

This world of chants, mantras, kirtan, satsang, angels, Bhakti yoga and the study of the Devi Shakti did move energy in my body, which truly helped my life. Energy healing, LIFT meditation and Bhakti yoga were the things I had been searching for. My cousin Kim, who wanted to help save the world by helping people as a lawyer, had found her soul had other ideas too. She had found her soul's gifts as an author and spiritual teacher, creating the Path of Ease and Grace seminars from her books and adapting energy healing into her own style of healing.

Opening my mind for one weekend changed my life forever, and straight away I could see how amazing energy healing was. The Path of Ease and Grace (POEG)[2] inspired me. So that is how the story, my story as Vikki, who found out her spiritual name was Devaki Ma[3], began. My soul family had a peace mission, and I couldn't be happier about that.

Later that month was the first seminar of Ignite Your Spirit (IYS) 1 & 2. It was all about the chakras and the aura. The book and seminar taught how to do an energy healing and LIFT meditation. I would be learning to give myself healing like I had experienced at the festival. All I knew was that we had chakras and an aura, and how good that healing had felt. I was about to find out what each chakra did in relation to one's body and life, and how to measure, clean and expand them with high-vibration positive energy. We were also to learn why we would want to do all these things.

When I first measured my chakras, I was not surprised by how small or non-existent they were. It was as if I already knew that my base chakra would be small or collapsed and that I was ungrounded. I already knew from the healing I'd received that my solar plexus wasn't healthy. We learned to feel auras and chakras with our hands using a method called scanning.

I was happy that I now knew how to clean and expand my energy body. I was learning new life skills through energy work. I was having fun; I always wanted to know more about energy work. Kim S Durga said it was just as important that the major chakras were all roughly the same size, because this made us more heart-focused. There was so much information in the *Ignite Your Spirit* book and the two seminars. We did lots of exercises in groups. It was during the groups when everyone was measuring chakras that we all learned how to do it. We could have five or six people finding the same size chakra, or similar type of answer. We all had a different way to explain it and sometimes no way to explain it, because none of us had done this before, let alone talked about it. These seminars gave us a common language to speak with each other.

At first this did not mean much, but later on, having friends who did the seminars with me was important. We shared much of ourselves, our lives, our feelings and emotions, and our passion for answers with each other during these seminars. We grew and changed together in unity, no longer alone in our separateness but surrounded by souls that were soul-family. We treasured each other's growth like we would any precious family member. Schoolmates are sometimes the best mates you can have, because they are going through the same things and can offer wisdom like no one else can.

As part of our journey, we were told to start doing what is known as spiritual practice every day. We were told how chanting could quieten our minds and still the endless thoughts that run through them. I would wake up chanting or find myself chanting when I was doing housework. This was good, because it kept me in the heart centre and stilled my mind. It stopped negative thoughts about myself and others. This was very helpful when trying to be mindful and not slip back into old patterns that were released in healings and meditations. Part of my spiritual practice was chanting as often as I could. Especially in times when I felt fear, or when my brain had endless chatter.

I also started listening to a CD about my solar plexus in a 40-day sadhana – a sadhana being a spiritual practice you commit to for a set period of time. Forty days is long enough for real change to happen. The more I swept my solar plexus, the better I felt physically.

I was connecting each day when I did the practices of meditating, chanting, cleaning, sweeping and expanding the chakras. Connecting more to my soul's self-healing, I stopped being a critical parent and started to spend time nurturing my soul's interests. Then I was in a better state to serve others, to find my path, my part to play where my uniqueness was needed. As I cleaned up more of my energy, I became lighter and clearer on what was authentically mine, not conditioning. I discovered how much self was not present but hidden in the thoughts and beliefs of others I was carrying. I found more self-love. The energy from the Earth and universe I felt through my connection to soul was pure, unconditional love.

It took courage to continue to clean and grow my chakras when I had been numb for a long time. I had hidden and forced down my fears and feelings in secret holes inside the energy body – the too-hard basket for my personality that was not equipped to handle negative information or the hardships of life. I just wanted the fear and pain to stop, so I could go numb again. But I was changing my mindset, discovering how much was not *my* opinion or belief, but one I was carrying from people in my life, past and present. As an empath, wife, mother and nurse, I had looked after many people and taken much of their energy into my energy field. When I started isolating other people's energy and releasing it, and pulling my own energy back, I started feeling again. I started loving again. I was discovering myself. The "myself" I wished I had the courage to be.

After the two IYS seminars came Yoga of the Mind from the *Child of God* book, which was about thoughts, thought-forms and beliefs. I was taught another great healing method for changing my thoughts and beliefs. Sometimes when we try to change things, no matter how hard we try, some thoughts and beliefs keep coming back. I learned that this is because the negative energy of a particular thought is still trapped within the energy body, in what is called the astral realm. The world of our thoughts and beliefs is humanity's free-will zone. Some might say it has been gifted to us, to play in or create from our free will our experience of life.

Again, the chants were very good at helping me stop the endless thoughts. I figured out that if I was chanting, then my focus was not in the astral world. I made it a practice of mine that whenever I found myself thinking, I would start chanting.

Empowering Relationships (ER) was the next seminar in the POEG course. My relationships with just about every person in my life were, to a degree, dysfunctional. I was a people-pleaser with no real boundaries. As an empath I carried lots of energy for others. Always seemed to take the blame on my shoulders for causing arguments. I was so bad-tempered and pushed to the point of insanity by others. I would say or do anything to get out of any fights. I did not handle conflict well. I felt no real love for myself or others; just fear. I felt trapped by love.

My relationship with myself and others changed to a degree each time I did this seminar. I started noticing that I was taking everything others did or said personally. I started setting boundaries, having those conversations. Stopped holding opinions of others, stopped feeling like a victim and taking the blame. I would chant away self-doubts and keep my mind from going to negative places, which can be an ongoing, never-ending process. At least now I had a method that worked for me.

MAKING PROGRESS

Once I started my practices, I noticed that my chakras were changing. The solar plexus, which had been huge, was shrinking to a healthier size in balance with the rest of my chakras and energy body. I was able to handle more and more situations without my usual stress and fears coming up.

Doing this energy work can unlock unconscious core wounds and beliefs. My first experience of an unconscious belief about myself that I had formed as a child was soon brought into my awareness for healing.

At one satsang, while in an energy blessing from a teacher, I heard the words, *"Why would the teachers let a beautiful young healer touch a filthy old thing like you?"* During these blessings, lots of energy came into my consciousness and chakras. My feeling of not being good enough to be around the young teacher obviously rubbed up against the container holding my old core wound. What did this mean?

I went for a walk to contemplate this and had a vision of myself as a small child, being told not to run around and get my good dress dirty. I didn't run around, but I fell over, ripped my dress and got it dirty, and I cut my face. I was in trouble, so none of my family present at the function were allowed by my parents to hug or comfort me. My parents didn't comfort me, and I still have a physical and emotional scar from this harsh lesson in self-comforting at about two years old.

As the energy came into my energy body, I was convinced I was a dirty old thing and that I couldn't be trusted to wear good clothes. I had learned I needed to self-soothe. I felt unloved and uncomforted, abandoned and unforgiven when I made mistakes. I also found myself feeling unsupported or unsafe around groups of people.

It was an accident when I had fallen, but my parents' anger and refusal to hear me formed the belief that no one believed in me. I started to review my life and thought, *Wow! I always worry so much about wearing white and other light colours.* I also had a problem buying new clothes; I felt unworthy of them.

This was totally unconscious to me until the energy of the blessing pulled it into my consciousness and made sense of it in my life. My parents had just been trying to control a two-year-old at a family function where there were many other kids the same age.

We don't know what is hidden in our unconsciousness mind, which makes up 95% of our brain activity. That means we are only aware of 5% of our mind and consciousness. The energy in music, chants and blessings has this way of helping connect us to the hidden parts. Once we are aware, we can choose to get a healing and change them. We can change the energy around them.

I started with a healing, but I also bought some new white clothes and started telling myself, through an affirmation, that *I deserved all good things*. I then heard my own scared voice say: "What if I get them dirty?" I could feel the fear in myself. I would answer: "*It's okay; we can wash them, or throw them out and get new ones. They are just clothes.*"

It was hard at first, but it helped that the energy of the original event and story was gone, lifted to a more positive level. I felt more loved and accepted by myself, which might sound weird and unimportant, but self-love was my light work at this stage.

After that life-changing blessing, I now love to dress up in good clothes, even white ones. I still tell myself when I spill lunch on them that *it's okay, we can wash them*. Before I did this kind of work on myself, I would have bashed myself up for spilling food. The reason we do this form of self-abuse is hidden in our energy body, waiting to be found. I am so happy I found a way to help the little two-year-old girl still trapped in that moment of suffering.

I still struggle to ask for help when I need it. I tend to not expect hugs when I am upset, so I self-soothe still. I can still feel unsafe around confident people and tend to hide my vulnerability behind anger or indifference. But it's at a deeper level of my unconsciousness and a higher vibration each time. I am healing more and more parts of my unconscious mind each time. Bit by bit, it has changed the way I love myself. The inner work was creating more room for my own energy, less for others. I was changing my lifetime patterns.

During the seminars, the teachers ask, "*What do you want in your life?*" So, I had to start thinking, *what do I want?* The exercises started to keep me honest. I started asking for things and then they started coming. My awareness was expanding and I was noticing more.

Half of the time I loved the meditations and purification methods, but then I would keep trying to run away, telling myself none of this was real. Then I would have a drama come up, but it didn't affect me the same way. I would feel anger for five minutes and think, *Wow, I really am at peace*, because my own anger would shock me. I would then start chanting or gave myself a healing, and the reason for the anger was witnessed, named and gone. It didn't need to be put away in a too-hard basket, or projected into a situation or onto a person; when in the zone, emotions and feelings just flow. What may have once taken a week, a month or forever to get over can be processed through the energy body and healed rather quickly.

The Spiritual Laws are a tool that make the healing process much faster and easier. Such a freeing feeling, to forgive and let go. It is very peaceful to surrender worries and problems to the soul and universe to work out. Life does keep pushing new situations for us to handle, but it's easier with healthy chakras.

My health was another reason I was so interested in this new form of healing. I had a bulging disc, and had just been told by the doctor that I had arthritis in every joint and that I would keep going until I stopped. In those days I was in much pain.

The fear and rage trapped inside my energy field was painful to release. It still is, but I remember that I wanted to feel this energy physically. I wanted to know if these spiritual concepts were real and could help our lives. My body was giving me confirmation that they were. So, I kept going, and soon my bulging disc corrected itself and I started riding horses again. A miracle, it seemed, through using this healing process.

Another outcome of this work was feeling grounded after a lifetime of basically being ungrounded. This method was grounding my spiritual being to the Earth. I was feeling so connected to the Earth, more compassionate and at peace in my body. I was actually feeling love for myself, comfortable in my own skin and life. I was being "human whispered". I never knew how to be a human being, not really – until now. I had never felt cared for until now, when I was accepted and belonged somewhere: with a group of people I could talk to about our soul missions and spiritual knowledge, without confusion, because we all spoke the same language.

The exercises in the seminars and books helped to show me where and what I needed to work on. I had realised that the change the world needed was for me to change. I had wanted to feel different, healthier, to help the planet and its inhabitants. I wanted others to feel this good. I decided I wanted to help animals with what I had learned in the seminars. I felt at this stage that my soul mission was to be an animal energy healer.

I did the seminars over and over for the next six years and many other classes after the Path of Ease and Grace. Each time I did them I looked at a problem in my life, using the course as a way of making the spiritual concepts I was learning real. My connection with my soul was now at a deeper level than I had ever thought possible. I could feel peace and bliss in my body. I felt so expanded in my body sometimes. I loved being myself more, had energy for my interests and my family. I started feeling grateful and thankful, less of a victim and more empowered. I could feel the love and I had a deeper connection to my higher self. I started feeling loved for my own uniqueness. I could feel the power in the chants raising my vibration; the energy transference in the blessings and my initiations was helping my soul connection to grow.

The good thing about a spiritual teacher who has mastered what we are learning is the golden energy they can gift to the student through light codes. This lifts the vibration, expands the awareness and opens inner worlds that others can't. It helps students to live the teachings, to anchor them in the physical body, which is the path to empowerment and enlighten- ment I am interested in. Remember: I was looking to find connection with the concept that my body was mostly space with light or energy moving around at high speed, making it seem solid. I wanted to learn how spiritual concepts could be felt; I was asking who I was and why I was here. I felt that now I was on an amazing journey to discover my uniqueness and answer my questions.

EIGHT YEARS LATER: 2020
THE WELLBEING INITIATIVE

In 2020, Shanti Mission, The Wellbeing Initiative was created. The Path of Ease and Grace seminars and meditations were moved to an online school.

The Wellbeing Initiative is focused on the health of clients. The healings are still non-touch and can be performed from a distance. A person presenting with acute or chronic health conditions can find relief through an energy healing meditation. A group of five healings over a short period can truly shift the build-up of negative energy in the affected area of the body.

The Initiative moved into a more clinical approach to emotional and physical issues, using metaphysics, offering doctors, medical professionals and veterinarians' healings, and working in unity with traditional care in a more mainstream way. Doctors began referring patients to The Wellbeing Initiative for help with depression and to have a healer assigned to them.

The Wellbeing Initiative pays many talented IYS therapists to offer these healings and tries to match clients with the best healer for them.

I received five healings on Zoom between 30th July and 10th August 2020. I felt so much better afterwards and my pain was gone. I am having another five healings, one per week, to continue to support my health until and after I have eyelid surgery.

This is my testimonial from the first five healings with The Wellbeing Initiative:

"In the last few years, I had retired from nursing due to debilitating, painful arthritis in my joints. I had also stopped driving due to glaucoma and cataracts. The arthritis pain in my hips and legs, along with severe leg cramping, was stopping me from sleeping through the night. The pain levels were 10/10. My eyes were blurry and extremely

irritated from the latest complication, which needs another operation to fix. I was feeling frustrated, hopeless and angry.

From the first healing my emotional state changed for the better and the pain left my hips and legs. My eyesight restored by at least 50%, and I could see better than I had been able to for some time. I can now sleep through the night, rest comfortably in bed, and am feeling great after the series of healings. I have decided to continue with regular healings to maintain this level of joy, peace and comfort in my body. I was like a new woman; the pain was gone and I really felt heard during the healing sessions."

Vikki Koplick, 14th August 2020

In 2020 my healing and self-realisation journey continues, helping me to connect with my soul and mission. I wanted to find a way to physically feel my energy body, the one made up of space and energy that moves fast but looks solid in shape. The hologram of my own body is an illusion. How, in theory, can the divine energy at a quantum level help me feel healthier, and how can I expand my chakras and raise my vibration? This type of healing meditation and the Bhakti yoga practice of chanting is helping me answer these questions and make my life better.

Raising my vibration helped. My clairvoyance

is sharper and I have become used to feeling, after a seminar, healing or meditation, like my factory instrument, my unique energy body, has been upgraded. The wisdom of my soul, flowing in as guidance, whispers in my inner ear; I have visions in my inner sight and feelings that something is speaking and showing me the puzzle pieces of a giant jigsaw. As my mission starts to manifest, looking back from 2020 to 2012, when I first thought I would love to help animals by using energy healing, is like looking at a different person. My consciousness has expanded a great deal from the late 1990s, when I first realised others had written books and were talking my language in the movement called New Age spirituality.

I have found a way to create my own soul mission. A journey like this is a spiral going around, building on what has been done, never starting at the beginning again or winding in smaller circles, but always rising higher. My mission in 2020 looks nothing like the start did. In the beginning it was just an idea. It feels like I did take one step by doing the spiritual practices, and the divine kept taking ten steps towards me. Together we built a ladder to the next part of the puzzle. Once in the flow, my soul keeps building and taking leaps into the unknown. Every day I know I am building on yesterday towards the goal I have set myself. Healing myself has made it possible for my soul to serve, and the following part explains how.

PART TWO

A MISSION OF LOVE FOR ANIMALS

FOUR

A MISSION OF LOVE WAS CREATED

Having felt the health benefits of cleaning chakras for myself, and leaving behind "not good enough" and "poverty consciousness" to a degree, I started looking for what my soul really wanted to do in this life. *Why was I born?* In my heart I still wanted to save the world through helping animals. I kept asking for guidance, praying for help; doing seminars, clearing fears and self-limitations. How could I help animals using IYS therapy and the tools taught in the spiritual Path of Ease and Grace?

Now that my energy body was holding a higher vibration, I wanted to change my life. I soon realised that by changing myself, my life did change.

To become an animal energy healer was the goal now. I started doing healings on my own animals. I had a vision to change the way we care for animals to include energy healings. I started using energy work in my horse training and care. I did many free healings for a local rescue group to help foster parents settle an animal, or new owners to solve teething problems. Still, I am only one person; many animals need healing, and there are many problems. So, I keep using my spiritual practices to ask for help. I found that once I started praying, I couldn't stop.

When I did a healing on a stray cat or dog, they did not have bright and bouncy auras and chakras. Nor were they happy when I spoke to them. Many were confused as to what was happening to them. But once I explained what was happening, once they were regrounded and swept, and had energy put in, they became a different animal. Animal spirits are very easy-going and service-driven; they are servants of nature. They are here to assist humans and each other. They are very eager. I love to speak to them, as they just get to the point. They are happy to be helped back to connection to unity and love, excited to be onto a new adventure, and so humble. I am in awe of an animal's capacity to love. Once their energy is balanced again there is nothing to forgive; they just pick themselves back up and find the inner joy again.

My skills for communicating with animals during the healings continued to improve with each healing. I started asking them what they wanted. The answer from many was "*What I used to have*", or "*Just love*". I would meditate on these answers. Did the horses I asked mean they wanted what they had had with a previous owner, or in another life? Then the horses showed my soul how all their lives are a continual journey to them. I had a realisation that what they wanted was unconditional love and connection to Earth.

St Francis spoke to animals and called them our brothers and sisters; he anchored this mastery of consciousness for others. His life has been a great inspiration to my mission and this book. It feels like I am following in his steps and I often call St Francis to help with energy healings.

I have dedicated my spiritual journey to clearing myself so I can serve the animal kingdom. This is how my mission of love for animals began. I jump daily into the unknown and follow guidance. It requires many, many moving parts to keep going, but as long as I keep praying, purifying, meditating, pulling in the energy and doing healings, I will be in the flow.

I try to keep in the flow, following the synchronicity and coincidences with trust, taking leaps of faith into my own soul guidance. Being willing to be vulnerable enough to change and start a journey where the ending is unclear, as I have been doing since that weekend in 2012 when I attended the Bodhi Festival. My soul was ready for its mission, ready to do the energy work, ready to start healing. Above all, ready to serve, to become an instrument of love and peace. To take my passions and life skills and find my soul's gift. My soul's vocation is to serve the divine, humanity, animals and the planet. To show how anyone can use their dreams, passions and spiritual tools to first heal themselves, then inspire themselves and others, and find their path to a mission or service project of their own.

Becoming part of the evolution of human consciousness as part of humanity. It can have a positive effect on the whole of humanity. Spirituality is not just a concept, but becomes part of everyday life. I wanted to help create a better world for my children; this book shows ways I have found to help. I might be one person, but I am someone and I am doing something. In fact, there are very simple ways to create motivation, devotion, awe and connection, to find the magic in life and a way to turn a problem into a place for inspired service.

I learned to concentrate on my own relationship with animals and nature. There were areas in my relationship with animals where I could use my gifts to do service. I was no longer looking to others to save me or for others to change; I was looking within myself for the change the world needed. I realised I was the only one I could change, then I could become an inspiration for others to be brave enough to be themselves. To find the mission trapped inside, waiting to awaken. To learn how to follow their dreams, to love and be of service to our world.

FIVE

ENERGY HEALING FOR ANIMALS

My vision is that all animals receive energy healings as part of their care along with veterinary care; that rescue groups might have energy healers they can utilise with each rescue.

Listed below is information about chakras and energy healings I have found interesting over many years and the hundreds of healings I have done. Many people understand the colours of the chakras and where they are in the human and animal body, but I am not speaking about them. I want to show a different perspective from my personal experience.

Because of the different sizes of species and the fact that I mostly do distance healings, I use a scanning method I have adapted to suit my style.[4] The intention is that the adjustments to ratio are done by the divine, as it is a divine healing. I imagine the size of an average blown-up balloon is the perfect size of any chakra I scan. Be it a wild animal, bird, cat, dog or horse, each chakra I scan is measured against the imagined balloon, compared against its size and the size of the other chakras. Are the chakras swollen, depleted or balanced in size? What is the quality of the energy?

When checking the size and shape, it is my intention that a balanced chakra scans perfectly round, the same size as the balloon. Chakras can be bigger or smaller than the balloon. The chakra can collapse in my hands or warp in one direction during scanning. Swollen chakras tend to warp; the energy is often hot and prickly. Small chakras that don't collapse can have a blob of concrete-like energy in them. Concrete-type energy shows it has been in there for a long time, and there could be other chakras involved in holding this in place. Each chakra and the aura are scanned, and I note which chakras are the most unbalanced.

For a basic healing, the first thing I do is give the aura a sweep and add energy; then give each chakra a sweep and add energy. I check the chakras in relation to the problem or heath issue. If there is a question the owner wants to ask the animal, I ask it as I run my hand through the aura, mostly at the heart centre. I hold my hand on my heart chakra to connect deeply, heart to heart. I tend to hear the animal or my guidance answer, and may have an inner vision, like a small movie. This is the way my intuition works, but everyone is different.

As an Enrolled Nurse and horse, cat and dog

owner, I have a pretty good idea of the body systems, and now, thanks to energy healing training, I understand the chakral systems too. I started adding pale green Oms, energy for inside the body: through the digestive system, the respiratory and circulatory systems, the heart, the blood, the brain, the endocrine system, the skin and inner organs, the bowels and urinary tract.

I found this most useful for horses. The first time I ever used it on an animal was for our horse, Bella. At the time she was an 18-year-old ex-racehorse who had had four foals and had been dumped and nearly starved a couple of times, passed around to many people until she was given to us. Bella had diarrhoea, so we gave her the treatment the vet advised and put her in a yard, as the grass in the paddock where she lived was long spring grass, too rich for her traumatised stomach. Bella recovered very quickly because we gave her traditional medicine and I gave her daily healings. I coated the inside of her body with pale green Oms and filled her chakras with energy. The pale green energy is similar to a pale jade light. It acts like an anti-inflammatory, energy antibiotic and antiseptic, then continues sweeping the negative energy out of everywhere. The solar plexus needed sweeping because it is the chakra that affects the stomach; it needed rebalancing.

After that, I found that every animal I worked on could do with a little inside-the-body work as well as the chakras. I decided I would offer two half-hour healings, which served animals better than one long healing. I would pray and ask for guidance as to when to do the healing, then wait until guidance came around; this time, if the owner wanted to know something straight away, I would connect and scan for information. If the animal wasn't ready for the healing, I could still measure the chakras and note the ones needing help. I liked to wait for the owner to send a picture of the animal and for divine guidance about the right time to do the healing.

Once I start the healing, as mentioned above, I give two small healings. Pets with depleted auras and chakras have energy added straight away to fill them and the sweep is left for the next day or so, depending on the divine and my schedules. Pets with lots of swollen chakras with dirty energy are given a sweep straight away without question, and another sweep is done the next day.

Listed below are a few findings about animal chakras I have discovered during the healings I have done.

BASE CHAKRA

I found lots of animals were ungrounded in their base chakra (base of the spine area) and through their feet. I started regrounding these animals. They started to celebrate the fact that they were grounded and thus connected to Earth again: Earth the mother, the sustainer of nature. Animals wanted what they had had before – a connection to nature, to Earth, where they were grounded, where they could feel the love. By being in a relationship with us, animals were losing their connection to Earth. Not to mention our beliefs and thoughts trapping them more and more into being what we needed them to be.

Strays and rescued animals are often confused because they are very ungrounded in the base and feet chakras, which could explain why they haven't found a forever home. When animals are ungrounded, they can spook easily and be scared of their own shadows. Shock pulls the energetic roots out of the ground. A healing can sweep shock out of their body after trauma or an accident.

Being grounded can promote a feeling of safety and belonging, which helps with the abundance of having their needs met. This abundance comes from being well grounded in the physical world by a healthy base chakra and feet connected to the Earth. This expands the energy body and gives a feeling of wellbeing, which attracts better life circumstances for the animal. Owners have reported their pet being happier after the healing, and during healings, with my clairvoyance, I have seen animals celebrating the moment they are regrounded and connected back energetically to Earth. Being connected again to Earth makes it easier for more energy to expand the chakras, which in turn helps balance the whole energy body. If all animals were more grounded, the animal kingdom may experience less suffering overall.

FEET OR HOOF SECONDARY CHAKRA

These chakras tend to be part of the base chakra's energetic roots system. Every animal I do gets a small sweep in each foot, then I put energy in with the intention for energetic roots to grow from the feet and base into the ground. Energy is pulled up from the Earth to expand the feet chakra, then pushed back down to anchor them like a tree in the ground. Usually, I do this after quickly sweeping the whole leg.

SACRAL CHAKRA

In animals, the sacral chakra is about their sexual activity, hormones and life force, which affects their health. It's also a good place to cut cords of attachment going to people, other animals, times and events. It's the same for humans, only we also have our creativity and our unfinished projects in the sacral chakra as well.

During energy healings it is good to sweep this energy centre and add energy to the life force. Sometimes I add pale blue to cool the chakra down if the animal is not desexed and has behaviour issues caused by hormones. Sexual energy can be turned into aggression, like an adrenaline hit. I find the sacral chakra connects to what is happening in the solar plexus. A very expanded solar plexus can have lots of aggression in it. A depleted one is lacking in life force. The chakras together can tell quite a story about what is happening for the animal.

SOLAR PLEXUS

The solar plexus chakra usually needs some attention in most animals, especially if they have never had a healing before. If the solar plexus chakra is empty and depleted, the animal might be being picked on by other animals in the home, pack or herd. If the solar plexus is huge and full of dirty energy, then the animal is possibly doing the bullying or bossing around of other animals. It is also the chakra for stomach issues, so definitely a spot to clean in cases of colic in horses or vomiting in dogs and cats.

The solar plexus is another place where cords of attachment to other animals, people, situations and events can be cut. These are energetic cords that can take away the animal's confidence and joy; they are like light streams going everywhere, draining the animal's whole energy body. Over-the-top aggression and fear can be triggered if the solar plexus is unbalanced or empty. In the healing, these cords are cut, the light called back through intention. Negative energy in the sacral chakra expands the solar plexus as well. The chakras work together to make the animal fight to be the boss of other animals, to disobey the humans in their lives.

When the sacral chakra is depleted it can be the cause of illness, which will deplete the solar plexus too. The animal will be attacked by other animals or become very frightened with a depleted solar plexus. Chakras will be swollen but have no positive energy in them. Sometimes, when energetic cords of attachment to the past can be cut during a healing, I have had animals bounce straight back afterwards, from looking like they are very sick to being back to their usual self in minutes. Some will even start eating again after days of being fussy. This is how powerful energy work can be. Getting the base grounded, the sacral bouncy and free of attachment, and the solar plexus shining like a sun gives animals a friendly, open and energetic temperament. They get along with others and are bright and healthy.

So, to recap: negative energy in the lower chakras has an effect on the life the animal will have. No energy in the chakras makes them lethargic. Too much negative energy swells the chakras with aggression. Cords of attachment drain their energy body and keep them stuck in the past. Healthy, bouncy chakras full of positive energy bring peace to the animal. They usually sleep well after a healing.

Chakras are connected to each other, so they can tell quite a story about the animal when you learn to scan them. The size, shape and feel of the energy can affect everything the animal does. I find when I can run my hand through the chakra, I feel heat, spiky energy or depletion, or concrete-like energy or sticky goo. I sweep it into a container of salt water and use breath to pull in positive energy from the universe through the energy field, using breath to expand the animal's chakras with pranic white, violet, pale blue or green. With the help of the divine, angels and spirit guides, I pull the energy in for them.

HEART AND THROAT CHAKRA

The heart and throat chakras are involved in communication. The heart chakra of an animal is usually expanded in love. But again, it comes down to the base being grounded or not, and having a happy home with happy human relations. With a stray animal, quite often the heart chakra will have "playing" on repeat inside it: "*I am just looking for love*" or "*I am looking for what I had before*".

The throat chakra, when blocked, can stop the animal being able to communicate the need for love. The animal will then do weird stuff to get attention and communicate its need for love. This is when they can shut down completely, becoming fearful of any human. They don't feel love for anything. The biggest cause of this is the base chakra not being connected to the source of unconditional love, the Earth. Once the blockage is swept out, the animal is connected to love again.

Animals are mostly in unity, except when their chakras are dirty, which happens more when in relationship with humans. We are slowly separating animals from Earth and Mother Nature. This affects their connection with the unity of their species and leads to confusion for them.

Humans hold bitterness and revenge, anger, hate, even self-hate in their hearts. Throat chakras can be full of unexpressed rage, so much separation from one's authentic, loving self. Animals are naturally energetically lighter in the heart, more in unity. They don't have as much unspoken energy in the throat as humans do.

When I communicate with pets during healings, I like to clear up the heart and throat chakras first. This makes it easier for them to speak and for my soul to hear them through the clear throat chakras, with our heart chakras in unity.

AJNA/THIRD EYE AND CROWN CHAKRAS

The Ajna chakra is known as the master chakra, because you can put energy into it to reprogram it and the chakra will send it into every cell in the whole energy body. Changing the energy in the master chakra can create miracle changes in an animal.

In most pets, the Ajna chakra can get dirty with the thoughts and beliefs the owner has about them, those statements we make about our animals in a habitual way. It seems to be a place where the animal is programmed by the owner. Also, through cords of attachment, animals can be still connected to the thoughts and beliefs of old owners. Animals tend to not have thoughts about themselves unless programmed in by a human – which is what our statements about our pets do: lock the animal into that way of being with the person who thinks and believes it. If others think it too, it becomes stronger and can cause many weird behaviours in the animal.

When I am working on a behavioural issue, I know I need to look at the Ajna chakra. I tend to do a few releases and reprogram the Ajna chakra with more positive thought and belief. Strays can have lots of old programming, so helping them let go of the past, to be fully present with what is happening for them now, is important. I quite often reprogram these thoughts and beliefs, but (and it's a big but), as the animal's healer, I can't get rid of this negative energy for long if the owner and those around them go straight back to thinking or believing the same things again. It is like goo hanging around or something set in stone, the same program stuck on replay.

We are in a relationship with our pets. This means our relationship has an energy bubble, or aura, and chakras, which is how our thoughts and beliefs can be programmed into our pets. We are energetically connected; therefore, it would be great if, in cases of really stuck energetic programs, the humans involved received energy healings too. I can only heal the animal's side of these relationships.

Another time when the Ajna needs healing from an owner's thoughts is when the animal has been sick before and the owner is convinced it's happening again.

On the way to seeing a veterinarian can be a good time to heal the Ajna of an owner's fearful thoughts and beliefs in the animal's energy body. This opens the possibility for hope and supports them until they see the vet. The owner needs to be open to change.

The crown is where the animal connects to the divine. If the heart chakra is full of good energy, the crown will be too, because inside the very centre of the crown is a replica of the heart chakra. So, through the heart we can connect to heaven, the divine, the angels and saints.

At the end of sweeping the energy out, I add energy. Mostly this is done directly into each chakra or into the master chakra, the Ajna, especially when getting rid of the thoughts and beliefs we were just talking about. Another way to fill the energy body during a healing can be through the crown chakra – the energy coming in through my crown from the divine, the masters, angels and saints. Firstly, into my crown, down to my heart chakra, down the arms and into the hands. Then out through my activated hand chakras, my energy body being the vehicle through which the divine blessing comes.

During healing work, the spirit of the animal communicates in many ways through the chakras that tell a story to the healer. The healer may invoke the divine, an ascended master, an angel or guidance they trust to assist in the healing; in many cases direct communication can be received. Sometimes the guidance heard doesn't mean much to the healer, but means everything to the animal's owner. Animals *talk* to the divine in all forms. The healer can talk to the divine; therefore this communication to the animal's spirit is more real than most of us can believe or imagine. When we let go of our judgements and have an open, childlike, enquiring consciousness, not a mind that thinks it knows all the answers, we connect through our heart to the soul and just receive the guidance. Practice, and giving ourselves the time to learn, makes anything better.

This type of communication is for the open-minded and humble. When we do healings on animals, we need to remember it is an energy healing. We are cleaning the aura and chakras as well as thoughts and beliefs around behavioural issues. We ask for help from the one unified field, the divine; then we are the vessel the healing comes through. The healer needs to have a clean, clear energy body themselves and a pure heart with the intention of being in unity with the one unified field. They need to truly understand that it is the soul in unity with the higher self and the unified field of the divine by all its names, not the personality of the healer doing the healing. In traditional medicine it is the action of the doctors', vets' and nurses' personalities added to the physical medicine that heals, although there are still times when even traditional medicine knows about the God factor (when the doctors realise there is a greater force at work, creating a miraculous healing).

In a divine energy healing, the spirit is brought back into balance. We don't always know what an animal may be trying to teach us, so we can't know where the healing must go. The guides we call in to help with the healings can, from the one unified field, see exactly what is needed. This is why distant healings using animal photos can be just as effective as being with the animal. I prefer to do distant healings. Trying to hear the story from the owner while the animal moves around can take up most of my attention. Keeping them still is not as easy. It is good to do healings directly when there is more than one healer, though, because as a team, we can handle the animal and hear the story easily.

I find it easier to connect to the spirit of the animal in a distance healing, because people talking makes it harder to hear the animals speak. They are less likely to talk to me, and if I pat the animal the conditioned mind of my personality comes back and my ego blocks the guidance. Energy healings on animals can at times be very complex, but the energy I pull in from the divine is intelligent and knows where to go.

During the healing I usually find the following: most animals have a huge or depleted solar plexus, and cords of attachment everywhere. The Ajna can be full of the owner's thoughts. The heart might be full of fear, bitterness, hatred and rage. The throat chakra can be quite hot, sometimes likened to being full of concrete and wires. I tend to treat this the same way I do the solar plexus: by putting in the pale blue energy to cool it down. I put the blessing in through the crown or Ajna and ask it to go where it needs to go. I put the pale blue energy directly into the chakras. This cools down and helps shrink the swollen, hot chaos. I use the pale green pranic energy in the body in the form of Oms, or just gentle pale green washing down through the body systems. The pale green acts as an energy anti-inflammatory, antibiotic and antiseptic.

I always fill the base chakra and see white energy roots coming from the four paws or hooves, deep into the ground and then back up to the base, expanding the base, then back down again. When this is done the animal is regrounded. They usually celebrate by leaping in the air or dancing on the spot like a dressage horse. How they love to be connected again.

Sometimes owners need time to accept what the animal has told them – like if the animal is going to die or wants to be put down because of pain and low quality of life. I agree with whatever the owner wants; if they want to keep fighting, I keep healing, unless the owner tells me it's time to let them go. I would rather keep fighting than give up. Other healers might not have a problem telling others "It's time, the animal wants to go", and that's why it's great to have a community of different healers. Success in some healings might just mean that the animal is blessed before they pass. These healings are for the spirit of the animal, which has an effect on the physical body as well.

EXAMPLES OF DISTANCE ENERGY HEALINGS

Blue Boy Distance Energy Healing

My daughter and I have many horses that we share. Blue Boy is one of them. He is a 16-year-old thorough-bred trained to be quite a schoolmaster. He has experience in competition for jumping and dressage. Blue Boy can be bossy to the other horses and wants all the attention on him when people are around. Previously I have given supportive healings to him during a very serious injury on his back leg, just before he was given to my daughter by a friend.

When I asked him if he wanted a healing today, he replied, "*Yes, I would love one of those.*" I scanned his energy body and chakras. Mostly his chakras were swollen and empty of energy, his solar plexus being the one that needed the most help. He was also un-grounded.

In an invocation prayer, I called on the divine mother and father and my team of masters, saints and angels to help, and went to work sweeping each chakra, pulling in an electric violet waterfall to loosen the negative energy in each chakra and sweeping it out into a salt-water bowl. I then added white energy to each chakra and his aura to fill in the spaces I had swept and expand them with positive energy. I pulled in energy from the unified field of those I called on at the start of the healing, down from above through my crown, sending half to the animal so I didn't deplete myself and got some beautiful energy as well. Except the solar plexus, to which I added pale blue to shrink, balance and stabilise. (In most animals the solar plexus will be huge, and it really needs to be half the size of the rest. When the solar plexus in a horse is huge, they will be full of negative energy and unbalanced. The solar plexus is related to the stomach, so a healthy solar plexus can mean a healthier horse all around.) I made a light sky-blue colour in the throat chakra through intention.

I went to the base chakra and the chakras on his hooves. All these were empty and that meant he was ungrounded – not energetically connected to the Earth, which does tend to deplete chakras. So, I swept each hoof and the base chakra, added energy and blessed the hooves and base; energetic roots came out and I pushed them deep into the Earth, pulled the energy back up to expand the base and hoof chakras, then sent the roots down again, growing more secondary roots from the main taproot. I then swept the lumps he had under his tail, which were not cancerous, using some pale blue energy to shrink them.

Then I took pale green Oms and energy down through the inside of the body into all the systems. Very often while doing this part of the healing, I can see negative energy in the body when disease is present. The negative energy can be attached to an organ, like it is depleting it by sucking the energy out of it.

I gained energy, and as I was helping Blue Boy, I

was releasing from myself to a degree while helping him release. I was pulling positive energy into my crown chakra using yogic breathing of energy into the top of my head, down the centre of my body, into my heart chakra, then down through my arms. I allowed it to come out through my activated palm chakras, keeping some for myself.

I asked for harmlessness, for the healing to continue for two weeks, and for a seal of pale blue energy to stabilise the healing. A gold mesh came down around Blue Boy's aura to protect him while he integrated the healing. Any mistakes I made would be corrected by the divine, and I gave great thanks for the divine help.

Then I made sure I put energy into the bowl of water to clean it. I then cut from Blue Boy by running my hand from the back of my neck over my head and down the front of my body, saying "Cut, cut, cut." I made sure my hand was breaking any energetic cords coming from my chakras to Blue Boy and from him to my chakras. I then washed my hands with soap (alcohol wash can also be used).

Dantae Distance Energy Healing

In the paddock with Blue Boy is his pal, Dantae. Dantae was also given to us, as a three-year-old unraced thoroughbred colt. His owner didn't want to pay the service fee so told the breeder he had died. This meant he couldn't get racing papers.

Dantae was basically untouched; on the trip home

he reared up in the float and was very stressed. When put in the yard he wouldn't let people touch him. Someone who knew Dantae before we got him told us he was a crazy horse, but we didn't agree. I went in with him, reassured him and handled him, and figured he was fine and would be a quiet riding horse. He galloped through a few fences one day, but didn't hurt himself. We found out a kangaroo had been coming to the agistment place overnight; obviously that was why he had gone through the fences. Not crazy – phew!

Then we had him gelded. I supported him through that with healings, and asked for the right action and timing for a peaceful procedure, which it was.

With the drought, we decided to cull our herd down, so Dantae and another horse found new homes. But then the girl who got him had to have an operation and needed to rehome him, so we took him back. Now he is with us until his last breath.

Dantae is now six years old. After I gave Blue Boy a healing, I thought it was only fair to give his paddock mate one too.

Straight away I could feel pain in the back of my heart chakra, which meant I was, as an empath, feeling his pain. I knew it was time to cut the cords going back to all the times, places, horses and people of his past. I could feel his energy and spirit asking, "*Why was I rejected and why were people told I died?*" and "*Why do people want to pass me on to other people?*". I knew it was time to heal this grief in him and to speak to him. I swept it out of his heart chakra and swept his solar plexus. I said some releases around all the owners swapping and told him he wouldn't be sold again. I regrounded his feet and base. His energy body was good apart from the heart and solar plexus, where this situation had sat. It was the right time to heal it completely. He knows he is safe and loved now.

At the end of the healing, I put a pale blue protection around the aura, as well as a gold mesh with electric violet licking the mesh like a flame. I asked for harmlessness and that any mistakes I made be corrected, and for the healing to continue for two weeks and the protection to stay in place while the healing continued. The blue energy and the mesh let positive and healing energy in and negative energy out, but wouldn't let negative energy in. It helped strengthen the energy that was put in.

I then gave thanks to the divine masters, saints and angels that came to help. I put more electric violet out through my hands to clean the salt water before I threw it out. I cut from the animal by running my hand from the back of my head down the front of the body three times, saying "Cut", cutting the lines of energy that were connecting Dantae and myself during the healing. Then I washed my hands with soap.

ENERGY WORK ON OUR RELATIONSHIP WITH ANIMALS

Energy healings can work in many areas of our lives and the lives of animals, because everything is energy. People are sometimes trapped in ways of being that make them and the animals around them miserable. They can't see a way out, feeling walled in, like nothing can ever change for them. The negative energy has formed like concrete around them. They then defend it; even if inside themselves they know it's wrong, they can't stop.

The hatred we send to abusers, and these people in hopeless situations, goes to the animal too. We must understand that it is in the energy we are directing, and we need to watch what our energy does. We need to be giving positive hope to the animal in trouble. We will be empowering change and asking higher powers to help us. Calling on our teams and friends in the spiritual hierarchy to help us smash down these walls. Releasing all our old thoughts and beliefs that don't serve us.

Trapped energy can deplete us and lock us into concrete to keep everything the same. Stories that remind us of a specific event in time can reinforce our beliefs. We all know if we think something long enough, it becomes a belief. If we believe that for a long time it becomes a core belief, and then it will be buried in the unconscious mind.

In humanity's relationship with animals, there are millions of thoughts and beliefs in the unconscious mind. Each time we lift ourselves up out of outdated energy, we are doing the world a service. Each time we give in and sink into a thought or belief, we are being human and part of the problem. When pets receive a healing, this can open the owner's awareness, showing them much of what lies hidden in their unconscious mind about the pet.

RELATIONSHIP HEALING FOR DOGS: MEDITATION

A couple of weeks before my dog Ellie passed away, she came and sat on my feet, something she had never done. I had just finished typing up some of the book about healing our animal relationships. I was guided to connect to my dog. I could hear Ellie saying she was happy I was helping animals. I prayed, calling on the divine and my spiritual guide team, my full soul presence and Ellie's spirit, the dog deva and all the nature sprites and devas to be with us. Then the mineral, plant, animal, human and angel kingdoms, Krishna, Shiva, Lakshmi, Mother Devaki for protection, healing and better relationships to all the kingdoms through divine grace. Then I asked for blessings, that all dogs be blessed. *So be it.*

I asked for my relationship with Ellie, all dogs and dog devas, all animals and realms to be healed of the energy overwhelm, delusion and obsession. What follows is a series of steps for those who wish to carry out a healing meditation with their own dog.

See a waterfall of starry, sparkling white-and-gold energy flowing down from the masters and angels, then breathe that into your relationship with your dog and all of nature. The release: "*I now release all negative energy from my relationship to all dogs and the natural world, through divine grace. So be it.*"

Never leave a void of energy. Breathe in fresh energy and see it flood through the energy bubble of the relationship with your dog and nature. Empty all the old energy that no longer serves you. See the energy of overwhelm, delusion and obsession leave your relationship. See the extreme energy of scarcity and worry leave the chakra bubbles of the relationship you have with your dog. See the connectedness of all your relationships and yourself as a blue light with a diamond light around it. Your energy roots going around the Earth, having diamond strength. See all the cells inside you becoming lighter. Pull the light into your heart chakra as you expand into the knowledge that the whole *Earth* is part of you. Keep pulling in the light until you feel all the realms are inside of your energy body.

See this blue light with diamond strength flowing into the relationship bubbles. Now the blue light is starting to shine and the meridians inside the bubble activate a rainbow light. Now a rainbow light with diamond strength is emanating from the bubbles. See yourself as a bridge of rainbow light. An ascended master (of your choice) comes to you and puts a sphere of diamond light in your Ajna chakra. Breathe in and hold; expand and breathe normally. You become a rainbow sphere on a rainbow light bridge that expands from where you have been to where you are going in the future. The bridge of all the endless possibilities of creation. As you connect to this sphere-shaped diamond on the rainbow bridge, you jump into the sphere and start to spin.

Rainbow light comes from the sphere and goes into your relationship with dogs and the world in all dimensions. The minerals shine brighter; you see the rainbow light shine on the plants and they thrive. The animals are thriving and happy, and you shine this light on human and animal relationships and hold a vision of peace and balance. Stop spinning; step out of the sphere onto the light bridge, then back into your Ajna chakra. Bring your awareness into your heart chakra and expand everywhere, seeing the beautiful energy you brought back being distributed everywhere in your mind, body and energy field. Breathe the energy down through your base and feet into the Earth. Notice your energetic roots going deeper into the Earth, more connected and stronger, at a higher vibration. Send more of this light into your relationship with your dog.

Now a golden mesh seal comes down around the bubble of energy and seals your aura and chakras.

Stabilise. Thank the divine and cut from the energy. Remember the upgrade and be mindful. Keep releasing the old patterns.

Repeat this meditation. It can be used for any animal relationship.

SIX

PRAYERS AND HOPE

Another part of my mission of love for animals is praying for them. I realised I have free will and faith, which I can use to help animals. Faith in science, nature, God, angels, the universal oneness or consciousness. What I am really doing is surrendering my free will just a little to ask something bigger than myself to help. I have tried it my way and can't see a solution, so I am handing it over to my version of a higher power and staying open for answers. Then I know I have at least tried something. I have done everything I can to help.

There are so many ways to pray. Most important is to truly let go and not be attached to how or if the answer comes. I trust that it will at the right time, place and vibration, through the right people doing the right thing at the right time.

I often add a positive affirmation to stop my mind from drifting backwards into the worry again. I say the affirmation as if it has already happened. Then when it happens for real, I give thanks and celebrate by doing a dance or a "Woohoo!". I never take it for granted and try to remember to say "Thank you". To acknowledge the help given and take the time to let it sink in with a celebration. I have found it important for my mental health to find joy in the small victories. Life is a marathon and can be very heavy sometimes. It's great for me to find the awe and joy of a child and let the mystery of my answered prayers be a magical moment of connection and wonder. A huge adventure built in my flavour, my language, just for my soul. I personally think it's just as important to acknowledge each miracle as it is to ask in the first place. To be humble and vulnerable enough to ask. Thankful and grateful enough to dance in celebration.

This makes my life one of devotion and fun. I can rise above the victim consciousness to become a co-creator of a better world. It stops the feeling of poverty consciousness for an expansion into true abundance.

Nature and animals are so special to my heart, and I need to acknowledge just how special sometimes. Praying is a great way to do this. I am not super religious or experienced in prayer writing, but it comes from my heart. I call to the universe, God, goddess, the angels, and the oneness responds.

Below are a few of the prayers I have shared on my social media group. The power of group prayers can create miracles.

PRAYER REQUEST FOR GRACE

Dear God,

Please help all animal lovers, animal carers and myself realise the grace we already have in our souls for loving animals. Help us concentrate on the love, kindness and great work we do. Please give us a sign in our lives to help us see reasons to be hopeful for change. Help lighten our heavy hearts today and every day. May we realise the truth of our soul's grace in holding a vision for a better future for the animal/human relationship.

Amen

PRAYER REQUEST FOR GRACE FOR ANIMALS

Dear God,

Thank you for the animals in our lives. Please bless them with your grace, now and forever. Please send your angels to all animals who need your loving embrace, today and every day. Please help us create a wonderful, joyful future for our children that includes beautiful wild animals and many pets.

Amen

PRAYER REQUEST FOR CHICKENS

Dear God,

Please help chickens be able to walk on grass in the

sunshine, and have plenty of room in barns overnight to be safe from predators. Help people buy free-range eggs. Help us end caged chickens through your mercy.

Amen

PRAYER FOR EARTH

Dear God,

Please help us all to stop worrying about what others are doing in their relationships with nature and animals. Let us find something to do to help our own relationship with nature and animals instead. Please help us learn to have more respect and gratitude for nature. To be more humble and feel unconditional love for ourselves in our relationship with nature. Please help us stop bashing ourselves up, so we can move forward into more kindness and peace. May we all release ourselves from the guilt, shame and blame in our relationship with nature and animals. Please help us release all the judgements around the human treatment of nature. Through the grace of our souls and the universe of possibilities.

So be it.

PRAYER FOR BALANCE IN WEATHER CONDITIONS

Dear God and Mother Nature,

Please help rebalance the weather on Earth in

places suffering from extreme conditions. Please end the droughts that are killing natural areas, farmland, animals and waterways. Please fill the creeks, rivers and dams of country towns in trouble with clean water. Please help our weather conditions become more moderate. Please help the people of Earth grow in awareness of the changes needed to bring back healthy animal habitats in areas of massive drought and soil degradation. Please help us realise the importance of leaving enough trees to create oxygen and water, to create areas that are the lungs of Earth for all of us. Please help our swamps thrive as the breeding grounds for life and the kidneys of Earth, and help all the systems of Earth be balanced and healthy. Please help the people of Earth clean up natural areas and allow nature to grow without impediment from us.

Through your divine grace may the Earth be blessed with all she needs to be healthy. Please help us show our blue planet Earth how much we love, honour and respect her and how grateful we are for all she gives us. Through our hearts and souls and your grace may these miracles occur.

Amen

PRAYER FOR SUSTAINABILITY

Dear Universe,

Please help the people of Earth to realise they are someone and can do something to help clean and heal our planet. Please help us realise it is our personal responsibility to help create a clean future for the generations to come. Please help the people of Earth show their personal love and gratitude by changing the ways they buy products and dispose of rubbish. Please help the people of Earth realise it is their personal responsibility to leave wildlife alone unless an animal needs help, and never to touch them or disturb them for selfish reasons. Please help big businesses change to animal- and environmental-friendly options; adopt recycling and reusing habits; and use new, innovative ideas to create jobs that will clean up our natural habitats. Please help the wealthy see that the need for a healthy planet is more necessary than investing in what is destroying our health and the health of animals. Please help the government see what the people want and put the needs of the people before progress. Please help us change from progress at all costs to sustainability in all areas of our relationship with the natural world, animal welfare and each other. Please help us all forgive each other and get on with what needs doing.

Through your divine grace and compassion, please help us remember the love we all share for our wonderful blue planet. May Earth be blessed with unconditional love by the people of Earth in every action.

Amen

PRAYER REQUEST FOR ZOOS

Dear God,

In your divine wisdom, please guide us into new ways of treating zoo animals. Please help us in realising that healthy animals need to be in the wild. That breeding to increase numbers can happen better when the young are released back into the wild from zoos. Help zoos be a great place for animals who can't live in the wild because of injury or disability to live the remainder of their days; a great place for injured wildlife to be rehabilitated because of the amazing knowledge of the zoo staff. May all zoos work in cooperation with game reserves and wilderness groups to expand and be well supported.

Together may we all realise animals deserve quality of life and are not just here for our entertainment. Help us care for them in a divine way, with right action and divine timing. May we learn to progress to the soul level in our human relationship with animals in zoos.

Amen

PRAYER FOR STRAY DOGS AND CATS

Dear God,

Please help all stray dogs and cats find a safe place to sleep, clean water to drink and enough food to eat. Please help them find kindness, caring people and healing when they need it. When a stray crosses the rainbow bridge, may they feel our love. Even if they didn't have a safe home in life, we know they are safe with you forever. Please let them know how much we honour their light, love and serving hearts. We thank them for showing us what true forgiveness looks like, for many a rehomed stray has shown us such forgiveness and gratitude with never-ending love that makes our soul rejoice. Through the grace of love may they all know our gratitude, and that even though we couldn't stop their suffering, we love them.

Amen

PRAYER FOR DEPARTED ANIMAL FRIENDS

Dear God and St Francis,

Please look after our animal friends who are no longer here. Know we still miss them; we still love them and wish they were here with us. Please help them understand they will always be in our hearts and part of our animal soul family. Please help us celebrate their lives, as we remember the joy and good times. Please help us forgive ourselves for anything we perceive was our fault in their care. Please help us let go of the pain of losing them, and may we feel the love always. Please help us offer our love to another animal, and may this love be bigger, because the precious one we lost taught us to love more. Please help us move on but never forget the love that was between us.

Finally, we say thank you for creating such beauty

and love, then bringing it to us. Thank you, oh thank you, for all of our pets. Through your glory and unity may our love be sent to our pets. Through your love may we feel it back in return.

Amen

YOUR PET

The hope to have the grace to be, in gratitude, I carry
emotions for thee.
I lighten your burdens, you are my beloved master,
I gladly serve, as you serve the needs in me. Together
we will heal each other.
The grace to be in your animal soul family.
Peace, and joy, to come into unity, to live together as
family does.
One life gone so soon, but what joy it was. I saw you
through life's journey.
You were there for mine to the end, your eyes full of
love and heart big.
You love me unconditionally as I knew you could.
"My pet, you are the best part of my day," you say to me,
"Coming home to your love at the end of each day,
Keeping me present, stopping me drifting away to the
past.
Stopping me worrying about the future.
Here in the now is where your love can be found.
My pet, I thank you, and the lessons you taught
I will never forget, yet you will always be part of my
animal soul family."
"Oh, master, oh, master," I say back to thee.
"Our family, our animal soul family, is so important
to me."

PART THREE

A SOUL RELATIONSHIP WITH EARTH

SEVEN

THE SOUL HEALS WITH NON-ATTACHMENT

When I was doing healings on pets, mine and other people's, I discovered most of us need a relationship healing with our pets. I certainly needed a healing with my relationship to animals and nature. I was part of a society encroaching on animal habitat.

What was taking me out of peace? Where was my vibration dropping? What was my energy doing to the animal kingdom and their habitat?

I first looked at my own relationship and how I could make it better with guidance from the soul and my spiritual tools. This involved focusing on Attachment and Detachment.

I discovered that I can become overwhelmed with attachment to a pet, to things being better in the world. I can even become attached to the world, staying the same in a comfort-zone cocoon. When this doesn't happen, I become detached and feel isolated.

I learned that attachment and detachment both need something outside of me to be created. They are limiting and create many emotions and stories that won't bring much joy to me, especially if I overdo them. I often start to become very controlling in my relationships. The opposite is that I become too detached from my life altogether, hiding my feelings, becoming numb. I have a fear of loving in case it doesn't last and I am abandoned. This leads to more detachment, which can get very depressing.

I start feeling like no one cares and the world is doomed, which can also lead to a sense of detachment. At this point I can flip again into over-attachment, which is when I start to get very angry at myself and look outside of myself to blame and shame humanity. Going from over-attachment to detachment and back again. Reacting over and over to the endless suffering of animals, arguing and gossiping about the causes of all the problems.

This is how, I have been taught to behave. Attachment shows I care; becoming detached is the way to cope when things don't go well. Accepting whatever happens by not being attached to a positive outcome has made me feel heartless in the past. I have been told I am heartless because I am not attached to a positive-only outcome, and that can be confusing. But being attached to the belief or thought that I, animals, the planet shouldn't be suffering causes the most suffering of all. Besides, I know my life is meant to be hard to teach strength, to drive me to the point of crazy, to teach trust and patience, to help me find my inner joy in all situations. I know that when I let go of my attachment to the outcome, I can then allow something new into my life and all my relationships.

When I look at my past suffering without attachment, I see how it helped me to become the person I am now. My soul strength can help me look at my present suffering that way too. I know that I need to go through this to be ready for the rest of my life. Quite often I learn great things during these hard times about love and about those I love, which are priceless lessons for my soul.

From witnessing the suffering of animals, my soul learns strength, faith, trust, discernment, self-belief, self-care, self-love; my gratitude grows for what I do have, and the animals I have in my life.

While I live in a body, I can create grace or karma. Just like I can use suffering to grow in strength or to fall into being a victim, looking for someone to blame. My soul knows every relationship in my life is created to be learned from, to pay a karmic debt, to be a step forward on the journey of discovering all parts of the self.

Soul perspective is a little like hindsight. If you look back on your life, the moments of your worst suffering may have led to the biggest changes. Relationship issues building up until they spill over into anger. Honesty leading a new way forward.

When my ego wants to hold on, my soul wants to let go. Suffering can be the method the soul uses, which leads relationships into their next chapter. I can see how certain times in my life I have suffered and it helped me become a better, stronger, kinder or more grateful person. I can also look at present suffering the same way through non-attachment as to what the outcome will be.

I have the strength to handle being vulnerable and not knowing when suffering will end or what it will change or create in my life. I have surrendered my attachment, but haven't fallen into becoming detached. If I surrender to accepting what is, then I am empowered by my soul's mastery and strength. But if I become detached, I become numb to what is happening. I become a victim, disempowered and distant from my feelings and emotions.

Having no expectations or attachment also allows change, and I can get into the flow of the energy of what is really happening in the present, an empowered being of light. My soul is my strength and greatest tool to bring peace. I can give that gift to my relationship with animals and nature and walk my talk. Be love on legs for the animal kingdom. The animals need my love, not my pity.

My higher self is usually in bliss and divine perfection in the unconditional love and acceptance of self. It sees everyone else as another self. In this dimension there is only love; the animals and I are one. One blob of love with no separation. I am looking into the eyes of creation itself. The combined energy of this love blob pulls the animal and me up in vibration into the bliss of this higher realm. I start to know that this beautiful animal's spirit is connected to my soul, and the love expands. There is a moment where I feel this must last forever. Attachment tries to lower the vibration again, but the soul knows the moment can't last because I am busy and must get on with the rest of my physical life. The authentic messiness of it all creates heart-opening experiences that cause emotions to surface.

The universe is connected to itself in the love between the animal and my soul. The love is bigger than both of us and it brings a contentment deep within. A deep longing to belong, in the unity of no separation, which is joyful, wholesome and nurturing. There are no words that get in the way to create cracks in trust. There is just love. A safe space for the emotional body, the purest part of my inner being, to be loved. I have allowed myself this time to experience the unity of deep love.

Like everyone, I crave love, and perhaps unknowingly I am not brave enough to feel or allow it to fully manifest in my human relationships. I am guarded until I feel safe enough to trust and be vulnerable. For these reasons I find animals the greatest way to feel and give love. I can become a little over-attached or detached from my pets, and they forgive me. This is a totally safe place to practise non-attachment.

EIGHT

FOCUSING ON MY OWN RELATIONSHIP WITH ANIMALS

I had to start to look for what would bring peace to the animal kingdom in my relationship with animals. Firstly, I thought, *Stop judging other people*, which isn't easy – I am still working on that one. I don't like to be judged by my family, friends or strangers. Starting the blame game and the shame game, getting arrogant because I feel better than the ignorant fools out there. If I am being like that with my mind and energy bodies then I am part of the problem. I am picking on the people picking on others. None of this is being mindful; it is being reactive. It is playing energy games to win the prize of knowing the most or judging the most things.

My mind is the only one I can change and maybe inspire others to do the same. The only relationship I can change is mine. I, like everyone, need to allow myself to change at my own pace and allow others to do the same, or I will be the bully. When I want so badly for the world to change, I need to remember: everyone has the right to stay in the comfort zones they made for themselves by the Law of Free Will. I can help inspire others by the changes I make. I also acknowledge the right of their soul to decide when and how they change.

Instead, I offer ideas to the world. I walk my talk instead of sitting there, judging and expecting others to change. What if they were expecting me to change and I didn't want to or didn't know how? How would I feel to be judged for that? My soul tells me I must remember this before judging others.

I realised we each have lessons to learn and life situations to practise in. Although I may have learned something new and it's my latest thing, it does not mean everybody knows or even wants to know. When my ego starts thinking I am the only one who cares, my resentment and anger start to separate me from others.

When this happens to me, I can feel the world on my shoulders. I start to judge other people's attempts to help as not good enough. This is when I have learned to connect through my heart to my soul. My soul guidance is to let go of the delusion in these thoughts and beliefs based in untruths. There are millions of caring animal people in the world doing great things, perfectly capable of caring for animals. I need to concentrate on my own relationships, noting that other people's relationships with animals are not my business. My soul speaks from unity and truth, giving me the confidence to move forward to do what I have dreamed of to help animals.

To bring in more positivity and light, I need to continue to purify negative energies from myself and my thoughts, beliefs, words and actions. To lift my relationships in a more positive way for more light and truth. To not bash myself up for being human.

I used to do a lot of bashing myself up for having thoughts, beliefs, feelings and emotions. For getting hurt and making mistakes and hurting others. This can also lead to me being critical of humanity as a whole group, forgetting those I love again. I had to ask myself: "Is being so hard on myself and others really helping animals?" My soul had been showing me that I was getting attached to my way being the only way. The answer for me, again: let go through non-attachment. Being aware not to separate myself through detachment but to see this as a choice point of healing in my relationship with animals.

As a nurse in my earlier life, I had learned through acceptance that having a body requires some suffering. I guess Earth is a classroom for every living thing on the planet. Animals are born, live in joy and suffering, then die by various means. They don't live as long as us. From my energy healings on dying animals when it is time for them to leave the world, I have learned they do it through acceptance of what is. I have learned animals are not afraid of life or death; they live in the now-moment in a non-attached way. This spiritual structure and level of consciousness gives them a joyful outlook, a carefree attitude. When I concentrate on my own relationship with animals, I can feel the truth in this awareness – my soul reminding me that animals are not victims empowers part of my relationship with them. They don't need me to pity them. They just need my love.

My soul reminds me I am only 100% responsible for my own relationship with animals. In any good re-lationship, though, I am not responsible for the actions, beliefs or thoughts of the person or animal I am in a re-lationship with. I can't do both sides of the relationship, which is why I see animals as my teachers, especially my pets and healing clients. In the past my ego would decide that animals are victims to the relationships they have with me and humanity. But my soul sees a sentient being who has a mission, a personal life, other animal friends and a secret life I know nothing of, similar to any human I am in a relationship with. My soul, through doing energy work, has really shown me this fact: animals are well aware. But sometimes we can't ask them, so we speak for them.

If I was going to use my soul in my relationship, I needed to start to communicate with animals. To notice my own relationship to my pets and nature, to honour and nurture it. To try to connect to my pets more often with joyful emotions. I don't want to slip into taking nature for granted and ignoring opportunities to send love. I want to step out of my usual awareness into my soul's strength, calling on my higher self to grow my consciousness in my relationship with nature and animals.

NINE

STOPPING CRUELTY THROUGH ANIMAL ACTIVISM

When we think of animal activism, it's very hard to focus on our own relationship. This tends to pull us out of our hearts and our peace, which happened to me in the last half of 2019 and first half of 2020. I was heartbroken about the Amazon burning, then Australia was on fire. My horses had fires coming towards them for a month. But I had tools of prayer and ritual, meditation and energy healing. I used as many as I could and participated in group prayer and mantras. As the fires approached my horses, the main fire was finally under control and back burning was done to the bush reserve behind the property. As an added bonus, it turned out the local fire chief and another fire volunteer lived in the same street a few properties away in each direction.

In 2020, the virus highlighted the cruelty in the wet

markets and the never-ending problems for wildlife. I was angry and worried, fatigued from caring so much. I thought it was time for us to act to change the laws. To donate more to the groups trying to stop money being made by treating animals in barbaric ways. We needed to put pressure on governments to change the laws and focus on sustainability in habitat care.

If I concentrated on my relationship with animals and followed the guidance discussed in previous chapters, I was fine, but there was also the work of activism. These seemed to be the complete opposite of each other, and this was where I stopped being at peace and started being confused. These lower vibrations tend to envelop me in doom and gloom. The fear, hate, judgement, unforgiveness, arrogance, guilt, shame and blame are low in vibration. The lower the vibration, the more falsehoods, half-truths and delusions; the bigger the lack of discernment and compassion. Depression and hopelessness traps us in that vibration. We become trapped in fear, stuck in the past with no solutions to problems. Then before we know it all sorts of stories are being played out around us to show us proof of our drama. The vibration we are resting in is what attracts the stories, dramas and situations of our lives. Through the Law of Attraction, we attract what we put out.

Most people understand the Law of Attraction. Like a balanced ecosystem, we attract what we need. We attract similar people to ourselves as partners or friends. We attract into our lives what we think or believe we deserve or need. There are many things in our lives that we have attracted due to unconscious beliefs or thoughts. If we want a different experience of life, then we can change into a person who would have that situation in their life. We can think differently. We can act differently and attract a different future than what would have happened without that inner work.

Karma is another thing that comes to us through the Law of Attraction. If we do good things, we attract good people and situations and have good luck. If we do horrible things, we may attract horrible people and situations to ourselves.

In terms of our relationship to animals, the Law of Attraction can help us find our ideal new pet. They are looking for us and we are looking for them. Circumstances, synchronicity, coincidences seem to occur to bring this about. Strays find a rescuer; rescuers find strays. Animals that are injured go to find help. People set up stables, agistment places and rescue centres, and other animal helpers find the animals that need them.

We set an intention, and through the Law of Attraction it connects animals with humans. We solve problems and evolve this way. Throughout the history of mankind's relationship to animals, we have made mistakes, corrected them and solved problems. Animal care has become more love-based; technology has moved forward. Veterinary care has advanced so far since modern technology was brought in to assist vets in their practice.

As we look after our health better, we look after the health of animals better. With so many of us healing our energy bodies, of course we want to do this for animals too. If we can find more peace, so can animals. If we can love more, we can love animals more.

One of the biggest problems is overreaction to what we see. Our words and judgements can be cruel and useless. Examples of this can be seen all over social media, where we see pictures of the ocean and animals with plastic pollution around them. This has people saying that humanity is more animal than animals, that humanity is cruel and clueless, that we are the biggest danger – on and on goes the human-bashing. The thing is, we are all just carrying on with extreme overreaction. What humans are we talking about in these posts? Ourselves, our partners and families? Oh, no – it's everyone else but us and our families!

We are all part of the problems we have created with materialism and a modern world. We are all part of globalisation and we use modern technology. We all get health benefits from doctors and hospitals.

We need to acknowledge the great humans who seriously love nature and animals. We all care in our own way and we are all doing our best to cope with life, starting to take personal responsibility for our footprint. New inventions and ways to help clean up our waste are being invested in by many government programs. We need to go forward, but there are many things we have that we can't live without. Everyone wants a good home, job, money, food, water; a healthy family, healthy pets and wildlife; medical support, like doctors for ourselves and our families, and vets for animals.

Children and animals died in the past from many diseases that the modern world can now heal. Yes, the modern world has created new problems, but that is the evolution of the human consciousness. We solve problems and create new ones to solve. Many humans do wonderful things to help us move forward. They do this out of love and compassion. To try to bring hope, some joy and peace to the suffering. Making manifest a mission of a higher vibrational energy from their souls and big hearts. Joining other people with big hearts who find an area they are passionate about and dedicate themselves to changing it for the better.

Let us all concentrate on them. Send our positive energy and even say some affirmations that help hold the vision for them. Pray for change and, when the opportunity comes up, let go of judgements that separate us and have compassion that pulls us into unity. We might think we are just one person asking "What can I do?", but we are all part of a huge group energy called humanity. What we do matters in our relationship with animals and nature. We are offered a way to help. We can lift our own emotions and energy from feeling hopelessness into feeling much more hopeful. We can also let go of fear and have trust and faith in humanity.

We can stop being overwhelmed by the weight of animals' suffering on our shoulders. When we use our souls (which operate differently) to join forces, everything seems to flow. The right people, right place, right time for a win-win situation. It happens when everyone is happily playing the part that feels right for their uniqueness.

TEN

SACRED ACTIVISM BRINGS HOPE

At Shanti Mission Online School, many of the classes offered provide much-needed information on our journey. In the community there is much unity between us, like any soul family. I found this to be the case when I was stuck wondering how I could be an animal activist holding space for change in humanity's relationship with animals and nature, but at the same time being empowered in accepting others in unconditional love.

Kim S Durga started a weekly online class in July 2020 with the intention to hold a vision of helping create clean air, water and soil. She introduced us to the concept of sacred activism for nature. The principles of sacred activism give me much hope for animals and their habitat.

Sacred activism stops the finger-pointing and acknowledges that we are all part of the group called humanity. It is about having compassion for others, not judgement. It gives us a new structure to move forward and forgive ourselves and each other. We need our soul's strength to love unconditionally and be vulnerable enough to admit to ourselves, in our personal and group relationship with animals, that we are part of the problem, and to truly believe we can be part of the solution.

Below are Kim S Durga's words from her blog about sacred activism.

Feeling Angry and Powerless?

When we become outraged about a situation that is evolving in the world, like deforestation and oceans being polluted, it is easy to forget our spiritual training, and even how to hold a vision of a higher reality. Our personal ethics and morality can be tested as we sometimes behave in precisely the ways that we abhor in others. We become judgmental and blaming. Even people who are usually loving resort to name calling and shaming. Our anger and sometimes even hate can emanate from us, sinking our vibration like a stone and adding more dense energy to the clouds of darkness that already pervade the consciousness of arenas of challenge and difficulty.

One of those arenas is the way in which we care for, or rather we have neglected, to ensure that the Earth has clean water, clean air and clean soil.

Sacred activism is NOT:

1. *An opportunity to dump, rant, blame and demonise people. It's not about becoming a zealous crusader who sees enemies and demons everywhere. We lose our normal human kindness and compassion working in that way. It doesn't help the issue and builds more ill feeling.*

2. *It's not about pacifism. Working in the inner sanctums of love based spiritual potency is an effective way to serve and make a difference.*

3. *It's not political. Politics divides. We work in a way which brings unity and builds bridges across party lines. We utilise the spirit that's already inside of us, to bring common intention to create clean water, clean soil and clean air.*

4. *It is not to be used in isolation. When we do this work on the inner plane, it's important to make changes on the outer plane too. To look at what can we do in our own physical and attitudinal lives to support the work we're doing in our class.*

Sacred activism is challenging because venting is so seductive! We love to complain and see the problem as being 'Out There'. Working with light and love to effect positive change is likely to require a lot of us personally. Our aim is to work through our anger and then to work steadily and constructively towards our goals, taking others on a journey with us towards something that we can all relate to.

We know that people are resistant to change. Truth

to tell, most of us are. We can raise our vibration to find doorways to a better future that we never knew were there. (Durga, 2020)

11 Principles of Sacred Activism

1. *Clean Water, Clean Air and Clean Soil are our objectives. We hold a vision that the world becomes cleaner, and nature more nurtured and highly valued by humanity all over the world*
2. *The oxygen we breathe comes from the trees and the ocean, upon which our survival depends.*
3. *Nature is part of the same unified field of energy and consciousness that we are. The same life forces that exist in nature are in us too. We are part of the 'one thing', the infinite spirit flows through all of it. It's part of us and we're part of it.*
4. *There's an unseen world that we're interacting with all the time, a world of causation. What happens in the physical world of Earth is largely the result of inner and unseen forces. With spiritual, metaphysical training you can start to become aware of those forces and work productively with them, to bring forth a more healthy, balanced, beautiful reality for everybody.*
5. *Once we start learning and applying ancient wisdoms, we may commune with the natural world more deeply than ever before. Sacred activism provides an opportunity for learning and healing for*

nature and ourselves. We can connect with the spirit of nature and make a difference.

6. *When the relationship between humanity and nature is unbalanced, or when humanity itself is unbalanced, it creates imbalances in the physical world.*

7. *Thought is a creative force. Our thoughts create our reality.*

8. *What we focus on grows. Rather than focus on the problem, this training and service work helps us to flip our awareness, focus and energy into growing the solution instead of the problem. This is particularly important when we're dealing with horror stories about what is happening with nature (or any other area in life where we may perceive a problem).*

9. *Arguing with people who have a different mindset is generally futile. They do not listen. Vitriol, criticism, hatred, blame and opposition – these things just make people defensive. They further justify their positions as they don't want to be seen to be wrong, feel judged or 'less than'.*

10. *Love is the key to positive change. When we can send love instead, people can have epiphanies and realizations from within their own being, that possibly what they've been doing is not correct for them anymore. People can change. It's only with an energy force as potent as love that we can bring this change about. Love can melt the hardest heart and open the most closed mind. Through Sacred Activism we will*

grow in strength and capacity for love. We're able to love things that have previously been unlovable to us. This is working together in unity and taking responsibility in the sense of oneness. This approach of unity consciousness is truly liberating and a potent force for positive change.

11. *Working on the inner plane with healing and relationship tools, we create change not just personally but also trans personally. We can change our beliefs away from powerlessness and separateness. Not just by raising awareness, but by clearing the blockages to change. We call our spirit and energy back from the problems and use it instead to influence positive change and solutions in the world.* (Durga, 2020)

WORLD SERVICE

Kim's list inspired me to add a few items of my own for my mission to help animals:

Soul relationship with animals is the intention.

Holding a vision in our hearts that we are included in all decisions about the care of wildlife habitat, wild animals and pets.

Animals depend on trees and the ocean for oxygen. Oceans are a habitat and food source for many animals. Animals are part of nature and the same unified field. Part of the unseen world, animal communication seems to be from an inner world where the spiritual part of animals exists. They speak to those with the ears to listen.

Applying this ancient wisdom in our relationship with animals can help us use our spiritual journey to heal the relationship we have with animals. We can learn to connect and communicate with their spirits.

If humanity is unbalanced, so is our relationship with animals, which will contribute to distortion in animal habitats and food chains.

Thoughts are a driving force in our relationship with animals. Our thoughts create the reality of our relationship with animals.

Sacred activism for animals isn't feeling hopeless and helpless, or turning animals into victims and humans into evil creatures.

I find the principles of sacred activism helped me realise there really aren't any good guys or bad guys in the world, just educated or uneducated people. This helps me let go of my anger and find compassion for others. We are all part of what is happening to nature. We can create energetic changes in ourselves, and that helps the whole of humanity. I really like the idea of helping create clean water, soil and air through my love. Through sending love and changing my thoughts. It seems like humanity can grow that way.

These principles feel lighter and more hopeful for a more positive outlook in the future. I aim to change my mindset and consciousness to sacred activism as the intention in my future activism for the animal kingdom. Instead of judging others, I can hold other people's relationships with animals as sacred as mine. This is world service, and it helps me personally because it takes away the need for my anger and worry about the future. I can see a loving way forward in the relationship humanity has with animals. I can heal my relationship with activism from disempowerment to empowerment, my emotions from hate to unconditional love. I will admit my ego does enjoy pointing the finger at others, but when it is pointed back at me, I need my soul to help me. I am still a work in progress in this, as I am sure millions of animal lovers are.

Kim has again given me the emotional and spiritual tools I need to make the changes I need to make within my relationships with animals. I can continue my mission of love for animals and stop falling into misery when supporting animals through activism, in order to understand and have compassion instead. To stay in my soul's strength and peace and not fall into helplessness and hopelessness.

The following chapters are ways we can use the principles of sacred activism in our own relationship with animals, letting go of the old, outdated, typical ways we are trapped in what sacred activism isn't as we respond to animal cruelty. We are changing from conditional love to unconditional love. I find this such a relief for my emotions, and I can feel more love and less of a need to go numb just to survive it. When I get angry and heartbroken, I lose my peace and I am no use to anyone. I can't pull in my soul's strength, and

I become isolated in my pain. It doesn't help animals for me to turn them into victims and pity them in this cycle. Nor does human-bashing make me feel love for anything.

ELEVEN

A SOUL'S SACRED RELATIONSHIP WITH ANIMALS

Looking at what sacred activism is and isn't tells us much about a soul's sacred relationship with animals. Everything in and around us is made of energy and has a vibration. Our relationships have an energy, which has a vibration too. Each animal, or group of animals, has a different experience and vibration with us and humanity as a whole. The higher the vibration, the more likely our guidance comes from universal wisdom and truth, from the soul being at peace and feeling love even when things go wrong.

Let's have a look at the history of humanity's relationship with animals. The most famous person who cared for animals in the 1200s was St Francis of Assisi. At that time the vibration was low in humanity's relationship to animals. Animals were used for food, clothing, transport and pack carrying. They were fed and kept alive as long as needed. Few people knew how to look after their health back then.

St Francis taught a very high vibration lesson to all who would hear his words, including the animals themselves. He said they were humanity's brothers and sisters and that they were loved by God. People did consider him crazy at the time, not understanding his notion of higher vibration. Later, he was sainted for his sacred relationship with animals and work with the poor. To continue his mission, we use our soul's strength and go into our heart's unity to make decisions at the highest vibration possible for animals and their habitats.

Imagine what we could do for animals if we applied vibration, focused on getting our energy body in as high a vibration as possible, then sent love to animals, holding positive visions and saying positive affirmations. Instead of spreading the lower vibration of hopelessness, fear and guilt, and shaming ourselves and others, *raising* the vibration, breaking out of the past and getting into the flow of inspiration by using our hearts and focusing on love.

One of the things about our soul is that it can love unconditionally and see wholeness, where our personalities tend to see polarity. Not both sides of polarity, either, because that would be wholeness. Rather, a one-eyed view coming from experiences, thoughts and beliefs. The next chapter is about how polarity works in our relationship with animals, which can sabotage our sacred relationship and land us back into judging others to be not as bright as us because they have a different opinion.

The soul sees polarity as an opportunity to grow through free will, through things happening because nothing is black or white but grey and full of opposites. In the soul, polarity is balanced in an exquisite, unique, creative, artistic life with one-of-a-kind experiences. This is the gift to the soul from the animal kingdom that the personality may miss if it is hung up on polarity and does not understand the choices and gifts this offers in our lives.

We can only feel the love and freedom we allow ourselves to feel. The universe is a very sacred place, full of magic and awe to the expanded consciousness, and relationships have endless possibility in them. Love is the only thing that matters, because the soul understands with compassion that everyone is different.

EXPRESSION OF A CREATIVE LIFE

Mother Earth expresses herself every way possible.
Her attempts she does not judge.
Some are lost, some are half done.
Mother Earth creates with unconditional love.
Wholeness is at her call.
Both creative and destructive, she holds on to nothing.
The form, it changes.
Everything is not made with judgement.
By compassion is formed.
A continuum, a spectrum of wholeness.
We judge as bad and good.
Mother Earth does not.
Every creature is made with the energy of love.
Some for destructive ways and others for beauty and love.
Life has a life within,
The energy to create not held by restraint.
Both negative and positive are magnetic.
This is the nature of Mother Earth.
Earth has compassion for herself and her creations, and a
plan as well.
Where the creations see problems Mother Earth sees none.
Mother Earth is the power to create and destroy.
She does not judge herself for being destructive.
She has compassion for all of herself.

Mother Earth created nature's beauty to enjoy.
She understands that creation cannot be sustained
forever.
Life is constantly moving and changing instead.
Never repeating itself as it expands and learns.
Beauty, a tapestry of never-ending joy to be found.
Knowing when the end is a new beginning,
A creative expression of life.
Mother Earth is being creative again.
Moving freely as a being of light.
Oh! What a glorious sight!

TWELVE

UNDERSTANDING THE WORLD THROUGH POLARITY

Wholeness of nature is creative and destructive. Because we are creators, we are always in these cycles of creating a new relationship with our world. Sometimes we just want to create and sustain it forever, which causes suffering and goes against the nature of the universe and ourselves. Getting carried away with our creation for too long will pull us out of self-love and into obsession. Once we become obsessed, we are stuck in it. We have moved out of acceptance of what is, in favour of extreme energy of attachment. When we become attached to the form staying the same, we suffer, getting lost in our thoughts and beliefs that aren't necessarily real. They appear real to us because we are deluded by our obsession, telling ourselves what we want to hear and see.

We are so obsessed that we ignore the elephant in

the room: the polar opposite. Someone else does see the polar opposite and states this to us, and depending on whether we are ready to hear it and act upon it, we will either ignore them, argue our point, or change our mind and thoughts on the subject.

As far as our animal relationships go, are we being realistic and accepting that things can't stay the same forever? Animals get hurt, they suffer and they die, and we die too. If this natural process isn't being accepted, then it's not being honoured, and that affects everything we say and do.

When we heal ourselves of all these one-sided extreme reactions and find acceptance in knowing the wholeness of creation, not getting stuck in one side of polarity, we change our beliefs and thoughts to truly acknowledge the gift of polarity and the free-will choices it allows all of life to have. We have all had other people box us into their view on us and our lives. Why would we box our animals into our views on them? We aren't seeing the whole picture, the wholeness, but drama instead, and we are not being helpful. We are not being open to the magic within to find the gift in the relationship.

As we heal our relationship with animals, they will continue to push us to be better people and bless us in thousands of ways. The easiest way to help animals is to love them. To be grateful, appreciate their beauty and honour their right to divine abundance of the true wholeness. To leave the one-sided delusion behind us, to be in *Heaven on Earth* in this human life, is to accept wholeness in ourselves and in everything.

If an animal was a stray, but found you and now lives an abundant life, then in the wholeness of its life, was it ever really a stray or a victim of poverty, or was it just on a journey to you? Remember the multi-dimensional beings we all are. To the physical self, the person that society conditions us to be, the animal is a poor stray and has probably been through hell with cruelty or lots of judgement. We have all this compassion for the animal, but no compassion for the person imagined person who made this animal suffer so we can turn ourselves into the hero who saved this animal from death.

The soul has something to learn from the situation of finding and helping this animal. So, would the sentient being that is the animal itself learn something through this relationship with this person?

The soul learns much from the experience; the heart chakra expands and the energy body relaxes. If the person is a healer, it's another opportunity to use their gift to do a healing.

Next, I want to look at happiness through polarity. Happiness has an opposite polarity: sadness. We are happy when something *makes* us happy. We are happy when we get what we want. Happiness can rely on outside influences creating the feeling of being happy. We are light when this happens; we share it around, but it doesn't last, because it has come from outside of us.

In our relationship with animals, we might be happy when we get a new pet. We are happy until our animal is hurt or something goes wrong. We become so sad when it is time to say goodbye to our beloved pet, because it doesn't last – even though before we got our pet, we knew the animal would not live forever.

After things happen – again, outside of ourselves – to make us sad, even if it is just the news on TV, we start feeling guilty for being happy when there is so much suffering in the world. Our friends and family tell us their woes and again we feel sad. We feel guilt or even shame when our family or friends point out the reasons why we must be sad for them or the world. We can start to become paranoid that if we are happy for too long, we will pay, because something bad will happen.

This can become quite a real fear. The fear keeps us trapped in being a victim of trying to be happy but ending up sad all the time; feeling so much empathy for others that we are forgetting our soul.

The pursuit of happiness outside of ourselves brings the polar opposite, sadness, and then we become a victim of polarity. We feel like we are on a seesaw, going up and down. We go between happiness and sadness. When we are happy, we become a victim of whatever makes us sad again. When we are very sad and totally into the story of what got us here, we often tell others about the thing or person that caused this sadness. We blame and shame them and find people who support us in being a victim of this. Then we see other people or animals as victims too.

We want every person and animal to be happy. To be in a happy forever home with no bad guys, no injuries, no illness or death. If any of this happens to them or us, then surely, they are a poor victim. Even though we know happiness and sadness are part of life, part of having pets, we still expect bad things not to happen to our pets or family. This is very unrealistic, unaccepting of the reality of any relationship.

The soul knows there is more to our relationship with animals than the physical life. The soul feels the joy of sharing this Earth with beautiful creatures. Souls accept the polarity in the birth, life, death and rebirth system. The soul doesn't live in a fantasyland where all animal relationships are perfect and last forever.

The soul knows we are all here to learn and heal the past. The soul doesn't see the death of its furry friends as a punishment. The soul even knows that cruel acts are not an accident but are planned to be a way to awaken the joy within. A case of "what can go wrong will go wrong". Attachment to life lasting forever the same, with nothing good ever stopping, is not natural. Nature shows us all that things are created, sustained for as long as needed and then destroyed. Nothing and no one are ever really destroyed, though – just changed.

Accepting this reality in our relationship with the

glorious animals we love frees us to be joyful. To enjoy the time, we have with them with no expectations that it will last forever. We are living in the reality that whatever relationship we have with this world changes minute by minute. We embrace the changes and the new energy coming into our relationships. We find the hidden joys, loosen our grip, relax a little and listen through our heart to our inner world. We become empowered by the truth that we only have now.

Adding up the years is more of a human thing to do than what a soul would do. A soul is surrendered to learning from every moment to be joyful. A soul knows when it gets a pet that it is a journey of love, not to be enjoyed in some distant future or forever, but now. The soul is in the energy of the experience. The energy of joyfulness at the experience itself, not trapped in the ego's negative view of polarity. The soul knows that if it weren't for the experience of polarity, there would be no free will, no opportunities to change or gain real strength – the strength to stay in the joy of animal ownership, even on the sad days. The soul gains strength through the challenges faced. Because the soul operates within the spiritual laws, in its mastery it has no attachment to the outcome, only the ways it can use the opportunity given by this precious relationship to animals to share love.

To heal our self-hate, to learn to love the unlovable, to learn to forgive, to have mercy and compassion is to learn mastery of self in all circumstances. The soul is not a victim but a student of life, trying to learn to become a universal citizen.

Those who only believe in the physical world will continue to believe half-truths and look outside of themselves, becoming a victim over and over, while continuing to turn everyone else into a victim too. Looking for happiness, falling into sadness and totally missing the inner joy and gratitude for having a life in the first place. The joy of adventure, the beauty of the experience of polarity is lost if we allow the fear in the personality to take over from any mastery the soul may have. We become stuck in suffering, the glass half empty, actually pursuing sadness with the unconscious mind and happiness with the conscious mind, which puts us in a fight for our life energy. If we put this into every relationship we have, the soul is ignored, over-ridden by the ego, which is brainwashed by a victim mentality and the corresponding truth we see around us.

Polarity is a good way to understand the darkness and light that make up the universe, our world and ourselves. We can learn from a positive or negative situation. Mother Nature creates polarity through her wholeness. She doesn't judge her creative and destructive phases. Nor does she judge her creations as good or bad. Mother Nature creates, sustains and destroys with equal effort. Imagine Mother Nature having a continuum of animals from the smallest to the largest. From the poorest, most suffering stray to the most spoilt. From suffering in harsh conditions to paradise. Nature creates, in the laws of polarity, economy and attraction, the right animal for the right habitat. We evolve because of polarity.

NOW

The new day breaks,
Another go at the drama that is life.
Putting us under a spell of not knowing
Into the day of the new beginning
That never ends, as yesterday becomes no memory at all.
As time is now and tomorrow is a hope for another go at now.
For now is the chance for change,
Growth and more love.
Now is where I am with you,
Waiting for you to be in the place of remembering.
Remembering home is a moment in time that never ends.

THIRTEEN

FLOW WITH THE NATURAL RHYTHM OF LIFE

Have you ever noticed how many animals forgive humans as a race when they get better after being lost, neglected or abused? Can we say the same thing about ourselves? Do we forgive the human race for that animal being lost, neglected or abused? Forgiveness helps us move forward, but it also helps keep us present in the now-moment. Truly, what is the point in going on and on about how this animal was lost, neglected or abused if the animal is now found, well cared for and retrained or rehomed? They are no longer a victim. So, we send love and gratitude to the human race. We start to build a bridge to forgive each other, realising none of us are perfect in our relationship to animals, nature or each other. Our level of self-mastery shows in our relationships.

While we are sitting in unforgiving energy, bad

things are happening because we aren't watching. We need to start watching, looking for a place to jump in as the right person, at the right time, with the right skills or mastery to help. Don't let anyone stop you from taking your place as a protector and healer of animals and their habitats.

This is unconditional love; we understand how we got here and why things happen the way they do. We forgive the past, others and ourselves through compassion and lack of attachment to outcome. The less we forgive, let go and surrender, the more stuck we become in the past. The more we forgive and love, the more freedom we have to move forward by fully embracing now. Self-mastery allows us to see ourselves and animals as part of the evolutionary flow. Life itself is a gift to be lived now, not in the past or someday in the future. It is all about the messy, scary, wonderful moments of adventure.

The rhythm of life can be easily explained as a series of coincidences and synchronicity. That means we have events and situations showing us what we need to know right now. Many say that's *just* a coincidence; others know it's the way the universe speaks to us. When this continues, other people appear at the right time to teach us what we need to know, and this moves our journey forward. When we learn the skills of our soul, we need to use them; synchronicity can bring that to us. If we are in the flow and ready, we will notice these gifts. We will act on the opportunity that has been brought to us. We will see the connection between the energy we put into our vision of something we want to create, and the coincidence that will help us take the next step of our journey towards our goal.

The events and situations brought to us in the flow of coincidence are usually for our divine good. We become changed from a person to whom life is a series of unrelated events, to someone who embraces connection to the flow of life. We end up in the right place at the right time for the synchronicity to continue. We are looking for guidance and we get it. We are asking a question and the answer comes to us as a coincidence, or as guidance in a meditation, which helps us follow our intuition and inner voice.

How is all this useful in our relationships with animals? That could be best explained by how we live now as a whole race in our relationships with animals. The greed of big business and political leaders has got us out of the flow of life. We have become numb to guidance towards that which is for our divine good. "Every man for himself" and "It's just business" are other ways to describe the way we see life as a series of separate, unrelated events. Numbness to feelings and emotions leads to political decisions and the actions of businesses not being seen to have a real effect on animals.

Our heart is our strength; it follows the flow from our soul. Imagine now if big business and political leaders were using heart and feeling their emotions, then making decisions from the wisdom of synchronicity. Imagine if they knew coincidences were real, a needed to be observed and followed.

The natural rhythm of life has a way of keeping on flowing, going in and around us. We may not see the changes happening. As we dream of fixing something our hearts can't bear to witness, we step into the flow with the right people, information, assistance, abundance and guidance on what to do next. Then the universe comes together, the stars align. We let the synchronicity begin and watch coincidence after coincidence bringing us everything, we require.

This will happen a different way for those not in the flow, because it will be for the good of many. It will fix problems in the environment instead of creating them. Then another major thing will happen: we will all become part of evolution. The evolution of human consciousness has been going on for a long time. Many people have been out of the flow during history, but many were in the flow. Many created solutions for problems, while others tried to stop change by judging the new concepts. We are part of history right now; we are living it. Future people will study our time and judge us on what we did to contribute to the life they live. Some of us will be the heroes that changed the world for the better.

Our souls are part of this evolution of consciousness, whereas our personalities tend to just want to survive, so we will do whatever it takes to do that. Businesses want to make a profit. Politicians want to create wealth and for people to have jobs so they can balance the books like good accountants. In past centuries, that was all leaders did: collected money from the people as taxes.

Some governments have acknowledged the need to change from fossil fuels to protect animal habitats, to find new ways to handle water better. To clean up the mess industries have made of nature and create new laws to balance the care of humans, animals and nature. Many people are planting trees and living their dream lives while being a positive change for the world. This is our time, our chance to create future events. Our lives can be graceful and lived in the flow of love in unity with the universe.

No one can do it for us; we need to be strong enough, vulnerable enough to know we don't have all the answers. To not know what will happen if we step into the flow and follow our guidance. Many people find an amazing mission in life and it changes the world. These people listened to their inner guidance and dared to dream, and when the opportunity came, they leaped into it. People are seeing animals in need and opening rescue centres, not knowing if they can keep going once the money runs low. But because they are in the flow, people help them and abundance flows to them. The universe is an abundant place and we are all creative beings capable of greatness. If we never step into the flow, we will never experience it.

The nature flow is another way light goes out into the darkness to lighten our world. I will use my mission as an example. I set out to learn to heal myself but ended up finding a way to help animals. My first dream as a child to heal animals has become a reality because I am in the flow. I wrote the first draft for this book as it flowed from my soul; it came fast, but then I had to edit it and break into different parts. I also had to educate myself about publishing, marketing and social media pages, and make a website to advertise my healings. Coincidences kept the right people teaching free webinars with everything I wanted to learn! Because it's a divine mission, there are many moving parts, and it is going into places I have never been before.

I am following my guidance, feeling vulnerable, sometimes confused and frustrated. But I know that I am in the flow and that I am building the foundation of my dream life. I am creating something my soul wants to bring to Earth. I trust and have faith that my partner, the divine universe, is working through my energy body and my mission. That technically it's not my mission, but a commission from the divine, a gift to my soul, not for my ego. It is service to the planet, to the animal kingdom and to Mother Nature.

Love is the energy that drives and inspires my mission. Love is the reason I dreamed I could say "Yes" when the universe called me into action. The daily spiritual practices, the meditations, the rituals and devotion I have to my angel guides, my faith in the God seen through many traditions. My love of the mysteries of consciousness. The chants and mantras that help my energy body to keep expanding, to be capable of holding more of my soul. These hold me when I feel negatively about my ability to write or to be successful as a healer and author.

Feeling the unity, I am building a higher vibration within when I trust the flow and have faith in what my guidance says. We all have something to teach, something to say, and when we dream and step into the flow, we find our voice.

If coincidences stop happening and nothing changes, we need to expand our energy and focus, change our intention, listen to our heart, dream big and follow our guidance when it comes. Sometimes we have reached a crossroads and a test is our next step. This requires inner strength and courage, but do it anyway. Animals are waiting to support us. The whole universal abundance will shine the way for us. We will feel our way and love ourselves to get there. We will trust and have faith in ourselves to be able to connect, with gratitude, respect, humility, love, to the unity all around us.

FOURTEEN

LOVE CAN SET US FREE

Everyone thinks they are entitled to an opinion about animals, but sometimes it can just be judgement or passive aggression. Sometimes the cruelty we see is real – too real these days – but sometimes it is just perceived cruelty, because we are judging different approaches to animal care.

We all have so many opinions about animals and nature, and we all know exactly what being judged feels like. Opinions can sometimes come from a place of compassion as well as judgement. Having compassion means accepting, allowing, surrendering, being at peace with something or a situation. It means having love in your heart when you see the ignorance in one who is learning, and understanding that growth has many stages. You have learned something great, but not everyone will know what you know.

The key is being mindful of every time we judge

and flipping judgement into compassion. One way is to look at your own life. Imagine someone was judging your relationship to animals, but you were doing your best. Then imagine if they could flip that and offer you their understanding and compassion; you would know they understood that you were trying your best. Imagine what it feels like to be doing your best, with much to learn, while everyone around you is experienced. Instead of showing you how experienced they are, they show you how much they love you. They are happy with your attempts and so proud of you. How good would that feel?

This is the opportunity offered in every moment of our relationships with animals and each other. We can just be supportive and understand that everyone needs to make mistakes to learn. We can understand that everyone has free will and learn to love the unlovable parts of humanity that haven't learned to be kind to animals yet. We can do that by being mindful, unattached to outcomes and surrendered in compassion. Let judgements be like thoughts that wash through, but don't stick to our loving selves.

We love this planet, its animals and each other. This is our truth. We are compassionate people with great hearts and love for animals. If we want our world to be kind and caring, then let us start with ourselves. We are the world, and the only thing in the world we can truly change is ourselves.

When we are being compassionate, we are acting

from our heart and soul. When we are judging we are acting from our ego. We have rubbed up against the edge of our soul's growth. This part of our life is our classroom. I believe that in learning to release ourselves from the grip of judgements, each of us is in a different grade in this class. Being mindful of this is a helpful reminder and really brings out compassion. We need to have empathy for ourselves and each other. This is how we bring Heaven to Earth.

We should also consider acceptance of suffering. Accept and surrender to the fact that animals get hurt, sick and pass. Some suggest that veganism is the only way forward, but this is a reality not everyone agrees with. We are all growing and learning to accept that the relationship others have with animals, even if we consider it cruel, is not ours to fix unless we have all the facts and can offer real help. If not, we should just send love, because love can heal the world. Through the strength of our compassion, we know everyone has their own flavour, beliefs, ideas and way of being.

When hearing about an animal in trouble, can we even stop ourselves from judging the outcome? We get so involved with our attachment that we miss the idea of a positive outcome. We miss the chance to share a final blessing with an animal before it passes. We miss the opportunity to share our words of love with them, to tell them how much we care or simply send them love. We are too busy ranting about the abuse or abuser to see the animal, the warrior being. Why?

Because we are judging an animal's life experiences, not through their eyes, but our own. We are putting our fear of the unknown, of death, onto them. True compassion is accepting, honouring what is and surrendering to the experience of life; no matter what is happening, there is peace in the acceptance of it.

To truly have compassion for ourselves, in our relationship to animals and in the part, we play in the group relationship we all have, is to see past the negative/positive to the balance of the whole experience of life. We are all part of being born, growing up, living, giving birth to the next generation, growing old, dying and being born again. This is the process, and acceptance of this causes a degree of suffering in our lives and animals' lives. What is needed is to have true compassion for ourselves and society as a whole. (Light workers work in this area to help to lift this relationship.)

We need to realise we have all this inside us, as do all other people and animals. Thoughts, beliefs and delusions run through our small minds, which are controlled by the solar plexus in relationship to memory. Past hurts, past mistakes in relationships – how many times does something happen with an animal and we go straight back into the fear of it happening again? This means we are stuck. It may be a different time, life or animal, but we get stuck in the memory anyway. We then fixate on another animal in relation to our thoughts and beliefs. In other words, we can get trapped in a place where the energy has been turned into a living hell, and it becomes a negative situation for both of us. The animal then gets sold or put in a shelter and the pattern continues. The energy is the same, but the story or drama is slightly different and confuses us into believing it's something new. We are repeating a pattern that has been triggered by the past. We can then uncover a fear or phobia. We can't always know what phobias others have about animals.

We have free will in the way we interact with animals. Love-based care for animals is more the norm than it used to be. It is through inspired individuals and groups that change happens. This is important if we want to raise the vibration of our experience on Earth. We need to see the beauty of the free-will choices we all have in order to decide what we love and what we don't. The universe offers the choice in the first place, otherwise who would tell us to love or dislike anything? The beauty of free will and polarity is that they offer us the chance of dreams, choices, chances, lessons, adventures. We can spend our time in love and not waste it on things we don't even like.

I love horses, but imagine someone else being forced to look after horses because they had no free will to be with the house full of cats they would prefer. Imagine if I had to be with a house full of cats that made me sneeze instead. Well, I would have both, but it's not practical, so I have one cat and heaps of horses. Through my free will I get to decide this, and I have no judgements towards people with a house full of cats and no love for horses. That's because I try to concentrate on my own relationship with animals. I know it is the only one I have free will over and the only one that is my responsibility.

FIFTEEN

MY FAVOURITE WAYS TO CONNECT TO NATURE

Below is a great way I have connected to nature and animals my whole life. Only now have I realised these are actually small meditations. I have written them down as a gift to help you connect to your relationship with nature.

MEDITATIONS TO CONNECT

1. BREATH

Sit or lie comfortably and breathe in slowly through the nose and out through the mouth. Breathe in again, relaxing the shoulders as you breathe out. Imagine you are breathing in oxygen from nature and breathing out carbon dioxide to nature. With each breath you are releasing all your tension.

Start feeling gratitude for nature as you breathe in

the oxygen. Appreciating your gift to nature, which uses our carbon dioxide for trees, plants and grasses. How amazing the gift of our breath is for nature. Enjoy the giving and receiving. Feel how, through our breath, we are one, not separate at all. Continue to breathe in through the nose, out through the mouth. Breathe in from nature and out to nature. Breathe in with gratitude from nature. Breathe out with gratitude to your body, feeling your service to the trees.

This can be done anywhere, anytime, and can take just two minutes. Can you feel the loving service your body does for nature with every breath? Thank your body for serving the planet and for receiving the gift of oxygen from nature. Take this feeling of belonging and being cared for with you to whatever you are doing next. Feel how useful you already are to nature with your service of breath. Add your love for everything. Breathe out your love and breathe in the response. Breathe in the love nature has for you.

2. SOUND

Notice the sounds around you. This is an on-the-move exercise in awareness more than a meditation. Retrain your mind to notice your senses – in this case, the sense of sound – as you are going about your day. Walking to the car, putting washing on the line. Walking to school or the shops. Notice if you are hearing nature. Take a few minutes to listen to the sounds of the wind, the movement of the trees, the sounds of water, birds and other animals. Just listen and feel the joy in animals. Feel the power in nature and notice these sounds in between moments in your life. Even though you are busy, there are brief moments of resting in the sounds of peace and connection. Make this a part of your day: to just notice the sounds around you. A mini vacation from thoughts and stress.

When you first wake up in the morning, listen to nature outside. Take a walk around your garden with your first coffee. Listen to the frogs in the rain. The birds and crickets. (You could also listen to CDs of nature sounds, but why, when we have the real thing to listen to?) The more you listen, the more present you will become, the less lost in your thoughts. Your mind will hear what is happening around you now. It will focus less on the past and future. Just *listen*, and start to feel love for what you hear. It's part of life, part of your life. Love hearing the birds in your area. The sounds of the beach near you. Of the forest or a waterfall. Of a farm or horse paddock.

When birds fly overhead, whether you are inside or outside, do you notice their joyful noise? Even when you are having a conversation or watching TV, can you hear birds flying over? Send them love and thank them for keeping you aware of the universe beyond your mind. This awareness can grow with practice. Sitting quietly can help you at first to connect, then you may be able to hear the sounds of nature from anywhere.

3. SMELL

With the modern world keeping us inside or in our cars, with pollution of our cities growing, we are not using our natural sense of smell very often. We are using artificial perfumes and air conditioning. It's important to go out into nature to areas that bring us joy. Maybe you love the smell of the beach, a mountain or forest, a lake or river, a freshly mown lawn. The smell of horses, a kitten or a puppy, rain or snow or flowers.

Once a week, on your day off work, take time to go find some part of nature you haven't smelled for a while. If you love the smell of rain, go for a walk in the rain. If you love the smell of horses, go see some horses. If you love the smell of the beach, go to the beach. When you can't go because you are busy, you can sit quietly and visualise the smell of your favourite part of nature for two minutes. Promise yourself that you will go smell the real thing soon and keep that promise to yourself. Include smells you love as part of self-care.

4. SIGHT

This meditation is to notice how much you see. This isn't about your favourite shop or building. This is about nature.

Part 1: What part of nature are you walking past or driving by and not seeing lately? In fact, check while you walk or drive: are you seeing nature at all in between all the cars and buildings? The endless people and things going on in your mind? Are you seeing animals and trees, noticing flowers on the bushes in your garden or close to your house? Are you noticing a clear blue sky on a sunny day?

Part 2: We connect to what we focus on and what we see. Look around and connect to the beauty of the natural world as often as you can. Go for a slow walk, a walking meditation to see your favourite part of the world. Be a tourist in your area. Drink in the sights of nature in your town. Take time to really look with love at every flower and tree. If you live near the water, walk by and look; drink it in with your eyes.

Part 3: Send love back to the plants and water like they are beings that you know, your friends. You have a relationship with them, so feel the connection through simply loving what you see. Be grateful you live so close to this part of nature. Truly feel the love within you when you take a few minutes to see your garden or street. It doesn't have to be longer than your usual walk. You can drive yourself to your favourite spot for your lunch break. Take time to see beautiful natural areas to unwind for a few minutes after work. Take the kids for a run along the beach.

5. APPRECIATION OF BEAUTY

This is a walking meditation of appreciation. Whenever you walk somewhere, notice the greenery. Notice the trees, flowers and animals and breathe them in. Smell the essence of the forest or the perfume of the flowers.

Listen to the sounds of the birds enjoying life. Water running, waves crashing, wind blowing. Take in the sights like they are an old friend you haven't seen for a while. Look at every flower on a bush, look at every cloud in the blue sky.

Keep walking until you find the perfect spot to sit. Then close your eyes and breathe in through the nose and out through the mouth. Breathe in the oxygen from the trees around you and breathe back out to them. Notice the smells around you as you breathe in and the sounds as you breathe out. Breathe in, then breathe out your appreciation to nature for oxygen, for the beautiful smells, sounds and sights. Then breathe back in nature's appreciation for you. Feel how much the trees enjoy your gift of breath. Feel how nature feels your appreciation of its beauty. Start to feel your love for life, for breath, for beauty and for yourself. Feel the love you have for nature and realise how much nature loves you.

Make your relationship with nature a priority, even for a few minutes each day. Like any relationship we work on, it will get better the more work you put in. The more you do those quick meditations, the more connected you will be, without it taking hours. But of course, if one day you find yourself wandering around for hours, looking and smelling, sitting and drinking in the beauty, then good; enjoy your time with yourself and nature.

When we were children we loved to wander

around, experiencing life without thinking about it too much. Why did we ever stop? Why not reconnect to this part of yourself? This can bring peace to your heart and feed your soul. Allow the mirror of this beautiful world to show you your own inner beauty.

Be in your private place within and truly feel the unlimited love you have found by focusing on beauty, breath, the sights, smells and sounds, the magic of nature. Feel it now, not next week or when you have got all the family sorted. Do it now. Take yourself to your favourite spot when you feel stressed or are having a bad day. Visualise it if you can't visit in person. Sit and breathe in through the nose and out through the mouth. After a while you can feel connected through just one breath, feeling like you are swimming in an expanded space within the self, which is the bliss of the soul. Breathe in and expand in the love you have discovered in your relationship with nature. Keep breathing in the love and out the gratitude, developing your relationship with Earth. Send your love down through your feet as you walk and feel like you are walking on a planet that loves you.

Notice how many times you have a positive exchange with an animal, whether a pet or birds and other wildlife you hear and see. Then see how many times you choose to ignore the chance to notice an animal or play with a pet. Just notice the feelings in your body when this happens. You might be walking outside but are really stuck in your head. Did you hear a bird call? Do you hear dogs barking? Just notice these animals. Thank them for reminding you to be present with awareness, not trapped in the mind.

Notice over your weekend how much time you spend with animals. Notice how many TV shows or movies you watch with animals in them, cartoon or real. How does this feel? Were you full of joy playing with your pet, or laughing at a movie? Did you let your inner child out to play, or did you remain a serious adult all weekend? Did you hear or see the beauty of nature? What was one encounter with nature or animals that made you feel connected?

By undertaking these meditations, you expand your awareness from just your physical world, using your feelings to connect with your heart. You are feeling your own love for your world and evolving your consciousness in your relationship with nature and animals. You have a whole new world ahead of you, if you have the courage and spiritual strength to let go of the past and hold a vision for the future. Don't give up and just keep on doing what humans have always done; evolve your consciousness. Let us focus on healing our world through being our joyful selves, loving our animals, enjoying nature and expanding our awareness.

GURU

They say you are not necessary today,
I can be my own guru in a way.
But I cannot love myself enough,
To pass through that hourglass to the higher realm.
Not without unity and someone else at the helm.
Someone who knows the way.
Who can love my soul even when my ego has got hold of
another day.
Through all of my hidden agendas and phobias, you love
my soul still,
Even when I scream back at you,
You love my soul in a way I can't do because I am in self-
loathing and hate.
Much is hidden from plain sight inside my unconscious
mind.
A guru goes there and pulls that out all the time.
Amazed to see it's in me, what in others I hate,
With more love a guru does change my fate.
A guru can be really just like my soul's mate.
A mother, a father of love, to help overcome all the hidden
self-hate.
In this unification and unlocking of my own inner gate.
A guru helps with the empowerment of my sovereign state.

What joys together we do await.
This royal, regal, divine hero and mate.
The guru of soul that some underrate.
Who helps me release all my horrible self-hate.
Helps me change my karma, my grace and my fate.

Light codes, activations, initiations and affirmations of love
calling back.
Chants and mantras and ancient rituals of devotion are sung
And gifted to put me on track.
Songs sung to my soul until my soul sings back.
So yes, I need a guru to help my soul before I fall back,
To help me release the heavy burdens I stack.
In exchange for my unity ascension pack.
A guru can help a disciple with all that.

SIXTEEN

THE EPIC JOURNEY CONTINUES

Over the last eight years, since being introduced to the guru tradition of Bhakti yoga and teachings about the divine mother, my life has changed forever. I have healed more things in my mind, body and energy body than I ever could have in a thousand lifetimes of doing this alone from a book or concept. A community of soul family in unity, a group to ponder the big questions and study the spiritual mysteries with, has the power to shift mountains and create miracles in each other's lives. In unity we help each other, standing in our soul power to connect to the ascended masters and archangels.

I have been living the teachings through the expanding of chakras and the energy in the chants – a direct experience with the energy of Durga through Kim S Durga's teachings and guided meditations. My relationships with my family and myself are better and

I am working on my relationship with humanity. I have the tools to support my health, to assist the traditional means I am already undertaking. I have found my unique voice and my soul mission.

I have discovered an interesting way to help animals by becoming an energy healer and running my own healing business. I have also discovered a way to help ease the pain of animal cruelty and the heartache the work of activism brings up by learning the concepts of sacred activism. This is still a growing area and something to work on as I move forward.

I have opened my creativity, writing poetry and books. I will continue to be a student of life, healing myself to be a pure channel of love and light, to do healings on pets and pray for all animal life. To hold a vision of love being the place from which all decisions about animal care are made. Of animal habitats being protected through the principles of unconditional love. To hold a vision that energy healings become part of veterinary care and rescue work. A vision that all animal carers, vets and rescuers receive energetic help by learning to meditate; receive healings themselves; and become energy healers for animals to add to their tools of healing.

It turned out that my soul had another way in mind for me to help animals than to be a veterinarian, and it has been and still is a very exciting part of my life. Best of all, I get to share this journey with my family, very beautiful soul family and great friends, and to form a deeper connection with nature and animals. To connect so very deeply to my soul and to God in multi-faith ways and rituals. To my soul, the divine is so big it can't be contained by one tradition or religion. As a child I wished to study all traditions, and thankfully I grew up open-minded enough to go on this epic journey of discovery that isn't over yet.

I have a real relationship with gurus, ascended masters, saints and angels. I have awakened many of my gifts. But the most exciting thing I have learned is true unity with the divine through breath and my energy body. Spirituality connects my body to real, unconditional love and bliss. I have learned to have confidence in myself and my processes. To love as many parts of my shadow and light as I can.

I have learned who I am. I am my soul, on a fantastic journey in a very eventful life to discover my soul's unique beauty and express it to the world. I have learned to be in awe, to have gratitude and respect for the divine inside myself that was speaking to me when I was a child, reassuring me that I was alright.

For now, I know I am on the right path to heal everything that would sabotage my peace. To surrender my egos control of my personality to the soul so I can radiate love and peace into my relationship with nature and animals. Play my part by being a healer, and express my soul's poetry to inspire others. So, watch this space, because the journey continues. Who knows where it will lead? But I know I will meet you there and we will fly home together, my friends.

FOOTNOTES

1. Kim had changed her name to Shakti Durga, only to change it again in 2019 to Kim S Durga.

2. Path of Ease and Grace (POEG) is a series of nine weekend seminars created by Kim (Shakti Durga), including Ignite Your Spirit, Yoga of the Mind, Empowering Relationships, Dimensions of Wealth and Spiritual Mastery.

3. Devaki Ma is my spiritual name, given to me at Shanti Mission as a way to connect to my soul's essence. Devaki is the mother of the Hindu God Krishna; she is in bliss no matter what is happening, and embodies Krishna's joy.

4. To learn the method of scanning energy for yourself, refer to the Path of Ease and Grace or books discussed in the early chapters as part of my healing path.

FURTHER RESOURCES

Energy Healings
To find out more about my healings and to book one for your pet, go to my website:
Https://amissionofloveforanimals.simdif.com

Facebook and Instagram pages
Vikki Koplick Books: facebook.com/poetvikkiko-plickbooks
@poetvikkibooks
A Mission of Love for Animals: facebook.com/amis-sionforvikki
@amissionofloveforanimals
Facebook Groups
A Mission of Love for Animals (Prayers, Meditation, Love): facebook.com/groups/3222099377807643
Sharing prayers for current issues in our relationship with animals, and spiritual rituals and meditations from my teachers. A place to be in the divine love we have for animals.

Vikki Koplick Distance Energy Healer:
facebook.com/groups/1094513460755929
Sharing information about healings, chakras and energy work.

Poetry Books: When I was a child, I dreamed of expressing my emotions in poetry, and now they flow through my being like a river of love, wanting to be heard. My soul whispers in my ear the guidance my heart needs to heal and grow. An understanding in the form of a deep emotional awareness, flowing from a place of all possibilities. The light language of my soul in form.

Vikki's first poetry book ended up titled *The Soul Whispers Poetry* and was published in September 2021. Comprising of Two Parts and Fifty-six Poems Part One: Worlds with words of the Heart about change and deeper connection. Part Two: Forgiveness beauty found which explores the nuances of forgiveness.

The Wellbeing Initiative
www.thewbi.org
To experience healings for yourself, connect with the great people at The Wellbeing Initiative. I highly recommend them for all of life's issues and to assist with any health issues.

There are also many lift meditations available on the website.

REFERENCES

Durga, Shakti. (2009). *Dimensions of wealth*. Cooranbong, NSW, Australia: Higher Guidance Pty Ltd.

Durga, Shakti. (2010). *Ignite your spirit* (3rd ed.). Cooranbong, NSW, Australia: Higher Guidance Pty Ltd.

Durga, Shakti. (2012). *Empowering relationships*. Cooranbong, NSW, Australia: Higher Guidance Pty Ltd.

Durga, Shakti. (2020). Feeling angry and powerless. Retrieved from https://shaktidurga.com/feeling-angry-and-powerless/

Durga, Shakti. (2020). The 11 principles of sacred activism. Retrieved from https://shaktidurga.com/the-11-principles-of-sacred-activism/

Fraser, Kim Louise. (2007). *Child of God*. Forres, Scotland, United Kingdom: Findhorn Press.

Fraser, Kim Louise. (2008). *Spiritual mastery*. Cooranbong, NSW, Australia: Higher Guidance Pty Ltd.

ABOUT THE AUTHOR

Vikki Koplick is a retired Enrolled Nurse and an energy healer for animals. She is also a clairvoyant, empath and animal whisperer, and is able to speak to the spirits of nature and animals. As a child Vikki wanted to be a veterinarian and a poet. She lives in NSW, Australia, with her husband, dog and cat, and has a grown son and daughter (with whom she shares many horses).

Vikki's spiritual journey has led her to find her soul's vocation and mission – "a mission of love for animals". Her poetry has been published in poetry magazines. "My Rose Petal Heart" and "Bitterness" were published in *The International Poetry Digest Monthly* in September and November 2019, and "My Rose Petal Heart" was chosen to be in the top 100 for 2019. "Australian Brumby Love" was published by *The Cambridge-Hall Poetry Journal* in July 2020.

Vikki is currently planning the next book in this series. *A Mission of Love for Animals: Living the Teachings*. Also, a series of small poetry books. The first is titled *Worlds Within Words of the Heart: The Soul Whispers Poetry*.

Vikki's first poetry book ended up titled *The Soul Whispers Poetry* and was published in September 2021. Comprising of Two Parts and Fifty-six Poems Part One: Worlds with words of the Heart about change and deeper connection. Part Two: Forgiveness beauty found which explores the nuances of forgiveness.

To find out more about this book
or to contact the author, please visit:
www.vividpublishing.com.au/sacredanimalactivism

If you enjoyed reading this book,
please take a moment
to thank the author
by posting a review.

www.ingramcontent.com/pod-product-compliance
Lightning Source LLC
Chambersburg PA
CBHW021158010426
R18062100001B/R180621PG41931CBX00025B/45